STORY
EARTH

NATIVE VOICES ON THE ENVIRONMENT

COMPILED BY

INTER PRESS SERVICE

D0068015

MERCURY HOUSE
San Francisco, California

Inter Press Service Third World News Agency, based in Rome, is an independent global news wire. It carries news, features, and special services on the human side of development and political change.

Published in the United States by
Mercury House
San Francisco, California

United States Constitution, First Amendment: Congress shall make no law respecting an establishment of religion, or prohibiting the free exercise thereof; or abridging the freedom of speech, or of the press; or the right of the people peaceably to assemble, and to petition the Government for a redress of grievances.

The Dutch Environment Ministry has backed the book project from the outset and provided a subsidy without which it would have been much more difficult to ensure its success.

Cover: Patzún huipil (Guatemala), embroidered neckpiece of a cofradía huipil representing animals and plants around the sun that gives them life. Reprinted with permission from Ethnic Arts Publishing, Berkeley, California.

Printed on recycled, acid-free paper
Manufactured in the United States of America

Library of Congress Cataloging-in-Publication Data
Story earth : native voices on the environment / compiled by Inter Press Service. Introduction by Gro Harlem Brundtland.
    p.   cm.
ISBN 1-56279-035-8
1. Human ecology—Philosophy.   2. Indigenous peoples.   3. Man—influence of environment.   I. Inter Press Service.
GF21.S76   1993
304.2—dc20   92-43609
                                                                          CIP

5   4   3   2   1

Contents

Contents

Contents

PABLO PIACENTINI

(Director, IPS Columnists Service)

Editor's Preface

The environmental crisis that has enveloped the contemporary world is one of the most dramatic consequences of the development model imposed on the planet by Western culture. That model, in turn, is firmly anchored in a scientific and technological base that has grown and spread throughout the West. After almost two centuries—if we agree that the Western model took root in the first Industrial Revolution—the degradation of the environment is now universally characterized as a threat to the Earth and its inhabitants, and is probably the most widely debated global issue of today.

But both the diagnosis and the search for solutions are defined within the framework that gave rise to the problem in the first place. Taking a scientifically oriented approach and waving the banner of self-sustainable development as the formula that will lead to salvation, more concern is given to rectifying the excesses and mistakes of the model than to questioning the model itself. Such an approach attempts to preserve nature against irreversible damage in order to serve the needs of future generations—it is a call for erecting walls of enclosure rather than radically changing the foundations of the model and its objectives.

Pablo Piacentini (Director, IPS Columnists Service)

That is why it is legitimate to draw a clear distinction between Western culture and the cultures of others when it comes to environmental degradation. The cultures of traditional societies have not had any noticeable influence on either the dominant development paradigm or on the deterioration of nature as a direct result of the application of that paradigm. On the contrary, traditional cultures view nature as sacred, and their value systems are light years distant from the consumerism that has dragged the environmental crisis along in its wake.

And yet, the points of view of traditional societies are absent from the international debate on the environment, and they are not allowed to bring any weight to bear on the decisions that are adopted. If we add to that the fact that non-Western cultures represent the vast majority of the world's people, it is clear that there exists an enormous vacuum, in terms of both participation and information.

The purpose of this book is simple: to give a voice to traditional cultures and their visions of Mother Earth, the relationship between humankind and nature, the values that underpin traditional styles of life, the effects of excessive exploitation of natural resources, and ways of facing up to environmental decay.

This book has been produced by the Columnists Service of IPS Third World, a news agency specializing in information on the countries of the Southern Hemisphere, on development issues and on North-South relations. In this context, the agency is as concerned with informing public opinion on environmental questions as it is with increasing global awareness of the consequences of underdevelopment and the unequal weight given the southern countries in international affairs.

The information that circulates at the international level is characterized by glaring imbalance, an imbalance in favor of the industrialized, rich North and against the interests of the underdeveloped

South—this is the reality that IPS's editorial policy has been designed to help counter, and it is this policy that has helped shape *Story Earth*, a collection of views of authentic spokespersons of traditional societies on the environmental crisis.

Rome, February 1992

GRO HARLEM BRUNDTLAND

Prime Minister, Norway

Introduction: Our Planet, Mother Earth, Is a World of Sharp Contrasts

Although our technological and scientific advances have created a world economy of huge dimensions, there have never been so many poor, illiterate, and unemployed people in the world. One out of every five people lives in abject poverty, the majority of them women, and forty thousand children die unnecessary deaths every day.

Although modern transportation and communication systems are bringing the world closer together, the economic and social gaps between us are still widening. Our knowledge may have taken man to the moon, but our mismanagement and overexploitation of the world's natural resources have brought life on Earth closer to extinction.

For the first time in history, human activities are having a severe, possibly irreversible, impact on nature and the living conditions of all the species on our planet. Global warming, depletion of the ozone layer, lack of clean water, extensive loss of species and biological diversity, acceleration of deforestation and desertification are all signs of the global crisis now approaching.

For generations, traditional cultures have lived in harmony and balance with the natural environment. People have managed to survive without compromising the ability of subsequent generations to satisfy their basic needs. Traditional cultures are generally characterized by their respect for and ability to live within the constraints imposed by nature. Such cultures regard the irrational use of natural resources as a sin.

The isolation of many traditional cultures due to physical barriers and differences in social and cultural practices has meant preservation of traditional ways of life. Their very survival has depended on their ecological awareness and ability to adapt.

Indigenous peoples are among those most affected by environmental degradation. Many of them live in areas rich in valuable natural resources. With the gradual advance of organized development into such areas, the groups living there have often been deprived of access to their traditional land and water. Exploitation of natural resources has disrupted the local environment, thereby endangering traditional ways of life. The legal and institutional changes that accompany organized development add to such pressures.

Interaction with modern society has often left indigenous peoples out of the process of general economic development. Social discrimination, cultural barriers, and exclusion from national political processes make these peoples vulnerable and subject to exploitation. Many groups have become dispossessed and marginalized, and their traditional cultures have disappeared. They have become the victims of what could be described as "cultural extinction."

Whether we believe that all nature is life, that every tree or bird is a reborn soul, or whether we regard nature simply as an economic resource, we can no longer disregard the fact that the crisis related to the environment and development will affect us all, regardless of where we live, what culture we belong to, or how affluent we seem to be.

Environmental degradation is a threat to our common security and to our common future.

The World Commission on Environment and Development was established in 1983 to address vital global issues and to propose a strategy for dealing effectively with them. Sustainable development—defined as a process of change that can satisfy the needs of the present generation without compromising the ability of future generations to meet their needs—became our vision and strategy for global change.

The concept of sustainable development, which has now been firmly anchored on the international agenda, at least in principle, requires a focus on global interdependence and on the close links between ecology and economy, between environment and development.

In order to reverse present negative trends, we must change the way our societies are organized. We must move beyond merely trying to cope with the rapid changes taking place. We must also anticipate and prevent environmental damage, and we must take control of our future by means of new and more active management of global change. We must demonstrate our willingness to think along new lines and have faith in our ability to shape our own future.

The World Commission firmly believes that it is possible to reverse the environmental degradation facing us. But this can happen only if we act together, both within and among nations.

Sustainable development is an ambitious goal that cannot be achieved by working from the top downward. Democracy and broad public participation are essential to achieve sustainable development. People must have the opportunity to influence and control their own lives and the living conditions of their children and families. We also need an informed and alert public opinion that can constantly exert democratic pressure on the political decision-making process and lend support to even the most difficult decisions.

The environmental disasters that have come to light in former totalitarian states in Central and Eastern Europe are a clear illustration of what can happen if governments protect themselves from public criticism. But the private sector, too, has a clear responsibility for the state of the environment, and closer contact between the private sector and government is essential.

We are beginning to realize that the nation-state is too small an arena for addressing regional and global challenges related to the environment and development. Global interdependence necessitates democratic decisions at the international level. We must find common solutions to safeguard our common future.

Acting together requires peace. Only through mutual understanding, respect, and solidarity between nations and ethnic groups can we take genuine responsibility for our common future. We must become involved, and we must be willing to share. To prevent conflicts, we must make a concerted effort to deal with underlying causes, such as poverty, injustice, and violation of human rights. As long as such causes of conflict continue to exist, we will not have a stable international society.

Our efforts must start with the fight against poverty. Thus we need growth, particularly in the developing countries, but also in the industrial countries. However, it must be a new kind of growth, one that is not based on overexploitation of natural resources.

Economic growth has long been viewed as the major indicator of development. The world economy has experienced unprecedented economic growth over the past four decades. In 1950, the volume of goods manufactured throughout the world was only one-seventh the level of today. We can move information and goods around the globe faster than ever before, and we can produce more food and more goods with a smaller investment of resources. Until now, we have viewed growth almost entirely in terms of numbers or annual percentages, without taking environmental concerns into consideration. We are now realizing that growth that causes environmental degradation is not progress but deterioration. We must reconsider what kind of growth is desirable and what kind of environment we want our children to inherit.

Environmental concerns must be integrated into every level of economic planning, performance, and accounting. A truly effective strategy for change must be based on a cradle-to-grave approach, from scientific exploration and technological innovation, through the cycle of production and consumption, to control of emissions and waste disposal.

The market alone cannot promote environmentally sound behavior. In our current economic system, market prices do not reflect the true environmental costs of exploitation, production, consumption, and waste management. We must therefore devise policies that promote technology and investments that are both environmentally sound and profitable. A more active use of economic instruments to benefit the environment will require an international harmonization of rules and regulations to avoid distortion of international trade relations.

We therefore need a new generation of environmental agreements in which we seek maximum environmental benefit at a minimum cost. By making environmental investments in countries or regions where the marginal costs of reducing emissions are low, we could drastically reduce long-range transport of atmospheric pollution. This would lead to a greater improvement in the global environment than if we had spread investments among countries with less pollution and higher marginal costs. We shall all benefit if we start by reducing emissions reductions where they cost the least. If countries agree on common environmental goals and targets, and on a harmonization of measures necessary to reach these targets, then it will be easier to move forward more quickly than if nations act alone.

The eradication of poverty is a precondition for environmentally sound development. And resource flows from the rich to the poor are a precondition for the eradication of poverty. This requires major changes in international economic relations and in current patterns of production and consumption.

International economic relations pose a particular problem for poor countries that are trying to manage their environments, since the export of natural resources remains a large factor in their economies. The unstable and adverse price trends faced by most of these countries make it impossible for them to manage their natural resource bases for sustainable production. In addition, protectionism in the north costs the developing countries far more than they receive in aid.

We need a truly global trading system, and we need new efforts to alleviate the crushing debt burden that leads to a reversal of world capital flows, currently moving from the poor to the rich.

Developing countries are strongly influenced by international economic conditions, but they are unable to influence them. Relations that are unequal and based on dominance of one kind or another do not provide a sound and lasting basis for interdependence.

The emerging international consensus that economic growth and human development are closely intertwined makes it imperative to invest in human resources. Human development requires a more equitable distribution of goods, both within and among nations. A redistribution of assets, including land and income, widespread provision of health and social services, and equal access to formal education, will all be necessary.

Traditional cultures are repositories of vast accumulations of knowledge and experience that link humanity with its ancient origins.

The disappearance of such cultures constitutes a loss for society at large, which has a great deal to learn from their traditional skills in managing very complex ecological systems in a sustainable way.

The starting point for a just and humane policy for indigenous peoples is the recognition and protection of their traditional rights to land and the other resources that sustain their way of life—rights they may define in terms that do not fit into standard legal systems. It is crucial that these peoples have their own institutions to regulate rights and obligations for maintaining harmony with nature and the environmental awareness characteristic of their traditional way of life. The recognition of traditional rights must go hand in hand with measures to protect local institutions that enforce responsible resource use, and this recognition must also give local communities a decisive voice in decisions concerning resource use in their area.

Protection of traditional rights should be accompanied by positive measures to enhance the well-being of the community in ways appropriate to the life-style of the groups in question.

As the World Commission stated in its report, *Our Common Future* (Oxford University Press, 1987), it is a terrible irony that as formal development reaches more deeply into rain forests, deserts, and other isolated environments, it tends to destroy the only cultures that have proved able to thrive in these environments.

The marginalization of traditional cultures is a symptom of a cycle of development that tends to neglect both human and environmental considerations. That is why a more careful and sensitive consideration of their interests is a touchstone of a sustainable development policy.

STORY
EARTH

JOSEPH BRUCHAC

(Abenaki/United States)

The Circle Is the Way to See

Joseph Bruchac is a storyteller and writer of Abenaki, English, and Slovak ancestry. He is an enrolled member (Band No. 3312) of the Abenaki Nation/Vermont. The Abenaki Nation is not yet recognized by the United States government. The United States government is still not recognized by the Abenaki Nation.

Waudjoset nudatlokugan bizwakamigwi alnabe. My story was out walking around, a wilderness lodge man. *Wawigit nudatlokugan.* Here lives my story. *Nudatlokugan Gluskabe.* It is a story of Gluskabe.

One day, Gluskabe went out to hunt. He tried hunting in the woods, but the game animals were not to be seen. Hunting is slow, he thought, and he returned to the wigwam where he lived with his grandmother, Woodchuck. He lay down on his bed and began to sing:

> I wish for a game bag
> I wish for a game bag
> I wish for a game bag
> To make it easy to hunt

He sang and sang until his grandmother could stand it no longer.

She made him a game bag of deer hair and tossed it to him. But he did not stop singing:

> I wish for a game bag
> I wish for a game bag
> I wish for a game bag
> To make it easy to hunt

So she made him a game bag of caribou hair. She tossed it to him, but still he continued to sing:

> I wish for a game bag
> I wish for a game bag
> I wish for a game bag
> To make it easy to hunt

She tried making a game bag of moose hair, but Gluskabe ignored that as well. He sang:

> I wish for a game bag
> I wish for a game bag
> I wish for a game bag
> Of woodchuck hair

Then Grandmother Woodchuck plucked the hair from her belly and made a game bag. Gluskabe sat up and stopped singing. *"Oleohneh, nohkemes,"* he said. "Thank you, Grandmother."

He went into the forest and called the animals. "Come," he said. "The world is going to end and all of you will die. Get into my game bag and you will not see the end of the world."

Then all of the animals came out of the forest and into his game bag. He carried it back to the wigwam of his grandmother and said, "Grandmother, I have brought game animals. Now we will not have a hard time hunting."

Grandmother Woodchuck saw all the animals in the game bag. "You have not done well, Grandson," she said. "In the future, our small ones, our children's children, will die of hunger. You must not do this. You must do what will help our children's children."

So Gluskabe went back into the forest with his game bag. He opened it. "Go, the danger is past," he said. Then the animals came out of the game bag and scattered throughout the forest. *Nedali medabegazu.*

There my story ends.

❖

The story of Gluskabe's game bag has been told many times. A version much like this one was given to the anthropologist Frank Speck in 1918 by an elderly Penobscot man named Newell Lion. This and other Gluskabe stories that illustrate the relationship of human beings to the natural order are told to this day among the Penobscot and Sokokl, the Passamaquoddy and the Mississquoi, the Micmac and the other Wabanaki peoples whose place on this continent is called Ndakinna in the Abenaki language. Ndakinna—Our Land. A land that owns us and a land we must respect.

Gluskabe's game bag is a story that is central for an understanding of the native view of the place of human beings in the natural order and it is a story with many, many meanings. Gluskabe, the Trickster, is the ultimate human being and also an old one who was here before human beings came. He contains both the Good Mind, which can benefit the people and help the Earth, and that other Twisted Mind, a mind governed by selfish thoughts that can destroy the natural balance and bring disaster.

He is greater than we are, but his problems and his powers are those of human beings. Because of our cunning and our power—a magical power—to make things, we can affect the lives of all else that lives around us. Yet when we overuse that power, we do not do well.

We must listen to the older and wiser voices of the earth—like the voice of Grandmother Woodchuck—or our descendants will, quite literally, starve. It is not so much a mystical as a practical relationship. Common sense.

Though my own native ancestry is Abenaki, and I regard the teachings and traditions of my Abenaki friends and elders, like the tales of Gluskabe, as a central part of my existence, I have also spent much of the last thirty-two years of my life learning from the elders of the Haudenosaunee nations, the People of the Longhouse—those nations of the Mohawk, Oneida, Onondaga, Cayuga, Seneca, and Tuscarora—commonly referred to today as the Iroquois.

We share this endangered corner of our continent, the area referred to on European-made maps as New York and New England. In fact, I live within a few hours' drive of the place where a man regarded as a messenger from the Creator and known as the Peacemaker joined with Hiawatha—perhaps a thousand years ago—to bring together five warring tribal nations into a League of Peace and plant a great pine tree as the living symbol of that green and growing union of nations.

That Great League is now recognised by many historians as a direct influence on the formation of modern ideas of democracy and on the Constitution of the United States.

I think it right to recall here some of the environmental prophecies of the Haudenosaunee people, not as an official representative of any native nation, but simply as a humble storyteller. I repeat them not as a chief nor as an elder, but as one who has listened and who hopes to convey the messages he has heard with accuracy and honesty.

According to Iroquois traditions, some of which were voiced by the prophet Ganio-dai-yo in the early 1800s, a time would come when the elm trees would die. And then the maple, the leader of all the trees, would also begin to die, from the top down.

In my own early years, I saw the elms begin to die. I worked as a tree surgeon in my early twenties, cutting those great trees in the Finger Lakes area of New York State, the traditional lands of the Cayuga Nation of the Iroquois.

As I cut them, I remembered how their bark had once been used to cover the old longhouses and how the elm was a central tree for the old-time survival of the Iroquois. But an insect, introduced inadvertently, like the flus and measles and smallpox and the other diseases of humans that killed more than 90 percent of the natives of North America in the sixteenth and seventeenth centuries, brought with it Dutch elm disease and spelt the end of the great trees.

Those trees were so beautiful, their limbs so graceful, their small leaves a green fountain in the springtime, a message that it was time to plant the corn as soon as they were the size of a squirrel's ear. And now they are all gone because of the coming of the Europeans. Now, in the last few years, the maple trees of New York and New England have begun to die, from the top down—weakened, some say, by the acid rain that falls, acid blown into the clouds by the smokestacks of the industries of the Ohio Valley, smoke carried across the land to fall as poison.

Is the Earth sick? From a purely human perspective, the answer must certainly be yes. Things that humans count on for survival—basic things such as clean water and clean air—have been affected.

The Iroquois prophecies also said a time would come when the air would be harmful to breathe and the water harmful to drink. That time is now. The waters of the St. Lawrence River are so full of chemicals from industries, like Kaiser and Alcoa, on its shores that the turtles are covered with cancers. (In the story of Creation as told by the Haudenosaunee, it was the Great Turtle that floated up from the depths and offered its back as a place to support the Earth.)

Tom Porter, a Bear Clan chief of the Mohawks, used to catch fish from that same river to feed his family. The water that flowed around their island, part of the small piece of land still legally in the hands of the Mohawk people and called the St. Regis Reservation, that water brought them life. But a few years ago, he saw that the fish were no longer safe to eat. They would poison his children. He left his nets by the banks of the river. They are still there, rotting.

If we see "the Earth" as the web of life that sustains us, then there is no question that the web is weakened, that the Earth is sick. But if we look at it from another side, from the view of the living Earth itself, then the sickness is not that of the planet, the sickness is embodied in human beings, and, if carried to its illogical conclusion, the sickness will not kill the Earth, it will kill us.

Human self-importance is a big part of the problem. It is because we human beings have one power that no other creatures have—the power to upset the natural balance—that we are so dangerous to ourselves. Because we have that great power, we have been given ceremonies and lesson stories (which in many ways are ceremonies in and of themselves) to remind us of our proper place.

We are not the strongest of all the beings in Creation. In many ways, we are the weakest. We were given original instructions by the Creator. Those instructions, to put them as simply as possible, were to be kind to each other and to respect the Earth. It is because we human beings tend to forget those instructions that the Creator gave us stories like the tales of Gluskabe and sends teachers like the Peacemaker and Handsome Lake every now and then to help us remember and return us to the path of the Good Mind.

I am speaking now not of Europeans but of native people themselves. There are many stories in the native traditions of North America —like the Hopi tales of previous worlds being destroyed when human beings forgot those instructions—that explain what can happen when we lose sight of our proper place. Such stories and those teachers exist to keep human beings in balance, to keep our eyes focused, to help us recognize our place as part of the circle of Creation, not above it. When we follow our original instructions, we are equal to the smallest insects and the greatest whales, and if we take the lives of any other being in this circle of Creation it must be for the right reason—to help the survival of our own people, not to threaten the survival of the insect people or the whale people.

If we gather medicinal herbs, we must never take all that we find, only a few. We should give thanks and offer something in exchange, perhaps a bit of tobacco, and we should always loosen the earth and plant seeds so that more will grow.

But we, as humans, are weak and can forget. So the stories and the teachers who have been given the message from Creation come to us and we listen and we find the right path again.

That had been the way on this continent for tens of thousands of years before the coming of the Europeans. Ten thousand years passed after the deaths of the great beasts on this continent—those huge beings like the cave bear and the mammoth and the giant sloth, animals that my Abenaki people remember in some of our stories as monsters that threatened the lives of the people—before another living being on this continent was brought to extinction.

If it was native people who killed off those great animals ten thousand years ago, then it seems they learned something from that experience. The rattlesnake is deadly and dangerous, the grizzly and the polar bear have been known to hunt and kill human beings, but in native traditions those creatures are honored even as they are feared; the great bear is seen as closely related to human beings, and the rattlesnake is sometimes called Grandfather.

Then, with the coming of the Europeans, that changed. In the five hundred years since the arrival of Columbus on the shores of Hispaniola, hundreds of species have been exterminated. It has been done largely for profit, not for survival. And as the count goes higher, not only the survival of other species is in question but also the survival of the human species.

Part of my own blood is European because, like many native Americans today, many of my ancestors liked the new white people and the new black people (some of whom escaped from slavery and formed alliances and even, for a time, African/Indian maroon nations on the soils of the two American continents—such as the republic of Palmares in northeastern Brazil, which lasted most of the seventeenth century). I am not ashamed of any part of my racial ancestry. I was taught that it is not what is in the blood but what is carried in the culture that makes human beings lose their balance and forget their rightful place.

The culture of those human beings from Europe, however, had been at war with nature for a long time. They cut down most of their forests and killed most of the wild animals. For them, wildness was something to be tamed. To the native peoples of North America, wilderness was home, and it was not "wild" until the Europeans made it so. Still, I take heart at the thought that many of those who came to this hemisphere from Europe quickly learned to see with a native eye. So much so that the leaders of the new colonies (which were the first multinational corporations and had the express purpose of making money for the mother country—not seeking true religious freedom, for they forbade any religions but their own) just as quickly passed laws to keep their white colonists from "going native."

If you do not trust my memory, then take a look at the words written by those colonizing Europeans themselves. You will find laws still on the books in Massachussetts that make it illegal for a man to have long hair. Why? Because it was a sign of sympathy with the Indians who wore their hair long. You will find direct references to colonists "consorting with the devil" by living like the "savages."

The native way of life, the native way of looking at the world and the way we humans live in that world, was attractive and meaningful. It was also more enjoyable. It is simple fact that the native people of New England, for example, were better fed, better clothed, and healthier than the European colonists. They also had more fun. European chroniclers of the time often wrote of the way in which the Indians made even work seem like play. They turned their work, such as planting a field or harvesting, into a communal activity with laughter and song.

Also, the lot of native women was drastically different from that of the colonial women. Native women had control over their own lives. They could decide who they would or would not marry, they owned their own land, they had true reproductive freedom (including herbal methods of birth control), and they had political power. In New England, women chiefs were not uncommon, and throughout the Northeast there were various arrangements giving women direct control in choosing chiefs. (To this day, among the Haudenosaunee, it is the women of each clan who choose the chiefs to represent them in the Grand Council of the League.)

In virtually every aspect of native life in North America—and I realize this is a huge generalization, for there were more than four hundred different cultures in North America alone in the fifteenth century and great differences between them—the idea of the circle, in one form or another, was a guiding principle. There was no clock time, but cyclical time. The seasons completed a circle, and so too did our human lives.

If we gather berries or hunt game in one place this year, then we may return to that place the following year to do the same. We must take care of that place properly—burning off the dry brush and dead berry bushes so that the ashes will fertilize the ground and new canes will grow, while at the same time ensuring that there will still be a clearing there in the forest with new green growth for the deer to eat.

The whole idea of wildlife conservation and ecology, in fact, was common practice among the native peoples of this continent. (There is also very sound documented evidence of the direct influence of native people and native ideas of a "land ethic" on people such as Henry David Thoreau, George Bird Grinnell, Ernest Thompson Seton, and others who were the founders of organizations like the Audubon Society, the Boy Scouts of America, and the whole modern conservation movement itself.) There was not, therefore, the European idea of devastating your own backyard and then moving on to fresh ground—to a new frontier (the backyard of your weaker neighbor).

If you see things in terms of circles and cycles, and if you care about the survival of your children, then you begin to engage in common-sense practices. By trial and error, over thousands of years, perhaps, you learn how to do things right. You learn to live in a way that keeps in mind, as native elders put it, seven generations. You ask yourself—as an individual and as a nation—how will the actions I take affect the seven generations to come? You do not think in terms of a four-year presidency or a yearly national budget, artificial creations that mean nothing positive in terms of the health of the Earth and the people. You say to yourself, what will happen if I cut these trees and the birds can no longer nest there? What will happen if I kill the female deer who has a fawn so that no animals survive to bring a new generation into the world? What will happen if I divert the course of this river or build a dam so that the fish and animals and plants downstream are deprived of water? What will happen if I put all the animals in my game bag?

And then, as the cycles of the seasons pass, you explain in the form of lesson stories what will happen when the wrong actions are taken. Then you will remember and your children's children will remember. There are thousands of such lesson stories still being kept by the native people of North America, and it is time for the world as a whole to listen.

The circle is the way to see. The circle is the way to live, always keeping in mind the seven generations to come, always asking: how will my deeds affect the lives of my children's children's children?

This is the message I have heard again and again. I give that message to you. My own "ethnic heritage" is a mixture of European and native, but the messages I have heard best and learned the most from spring from this native soil.

If someone as small and pitiful as I am can learn from those ancient messages and speak well enough to touch the lives of others, then it seems to me that any human being—native or nonnative—has the ability to listen and to learn. It is because of that belief that I share these words, for all the people of the Earth.

TANIEN (DANIEL) ASHINI

(Natassinan/Canada)

We Have Been Pushed to the Edge of a Cliff

"What will you leave me, Grandfather?"

"All of my territory with everything you find on it.
All kinds of animals, fish, trees, all the rivers,
that is the heritage I leave you.
Down through the generations
this is what you will need for survival.

Don't ever forget what I am going to tell you.
During your lifetime do as I do—respect all the animals,
don't ever make them suffer before you kill them,
don't ever waste anything by killing more than you need,
and don't ever try to keep an animal in captivity
because the animals are necessary for the survival
of future generations."

> —A dying Innu man to his grandson, from
> *Qu'as-tu fait de mon pays?* by Antane Kapesh

Daniel Ashini is part of the first generation of Innu to be born in the community of Sheshatshiu. Before that, all Innu were born Nutshimit—in the country—where Innu have hunted and gathered since time immemorial. Sheshatshiu was just a summer trading place, until the government convinced and coerced the Innu into settling the village—and then began to plunder the land.

Ashini did the things that government authorities said would lead to a good life. He stayed in the community, went to school, then got a job as an administrator for the Band Council. From 1985 to 1991 he was chief.

Village life continued to worsen, and for the Innu who went Nutshimit, *the advent of military low-level flying threatened to destroy the hunting way of life. As chief, Ashini realized that the letters and meetings with government officials were going nowhere. The Innu began a program of nonviolent action, occupying military runways, blocking logging roads, opposing massive hydroelectric dams. Ashini played a major part in these efforts.*

At the same time, Ashini and others realized the importance of living Nutshimit. *Now director of Innu Rights and Environment for Innu Nation, Ashini makes sure that each year he goes* Nutshimit *for several months. This time gives him the strength and peace of mind to carry on a struggle that as yet shows no sign of ending.*

My people refer to Labrador and eastern Quebec as Nitassinan, and it is our homeland. Many Innu people continue to hunt, trap, and fish there. We believe that if we do not keep the door open to the hunting way of life we will be nothing as a people.

When we are in the country we are healthy, happy, and stronger—physically and spiritually. We escape the terrible problems of alcohol abuse, family violence, and attempted suicides that are making our lives in the village utter and complete hell.

In the country we do things that are meaningful, that enrich us, that give us pride and enhance our self-esteem. Our children respect us there. We work hard in the country and are extremely productive. Life there contrasts greatly with the misery of life in our villages.

We are also able to practice our traditional religion in the country. This religion is based on a belief in animal masters and other forest spirits. When we hunt we must show respect for the animal masters. We place the bones of the caribou, bear, marten, mink, and other creatures in tree platforms so the dogs do not eat them. We do not overhunt or overtrap areas where animals are scarce. If we do not show respect in this way, the animal masters get angry and punish us by not giving us any animals at a later date. Our elders communicate with the animal masters through dreams, drumming, steam tents, and a form of divination ccalled *matnikashaucu.* A caribou or porcupine shoulder blade is placed in the fire until it is charred and cracked. We read the marks to discover the future location of game.

Our hunting culture thrives in the bush. We do things that very few non-Innu know anything about. Nonnatives think they know us because they see us in their stores and at their hockey rinks, but they don't realize that there is another side to us, a side they would have trouble understanding unless they spent time with us in the bush.

We go to the bush for the kind of spiritual tranquillity that many others associate with their churches. But now the noise of low-flying jet bombers has destroyed our peace of mind in the bush. The jets startle us, terrify our children, frighten our animals, and pollute the waterways. They fly into river valleys, over lakes and marsh areas— places that are also best for hunting, trapping, and fishing. Our harvesting areas overlap with the military low-flying routes to a great extent.

How can the Innu people survive increases in low-level flying, the sonic booms created when jets rehearse air-to-air combat, the loss of more land to bombing ranges, the military sports hunters, the sexual abuse of young Innu women who live near the base, and so on? I think it will be very hard, if not impossible for us to continue our hunting culture if military expansion continues.

The Canadian government tells us we should compromise. Chambers of commerce tell us we should compromise. We are accused of being selfish if we do not.

Well, we think we have made enough compromises. We compromised when some off our best hunting and trapping territory was flooded at Mishikamau Lake to make the Smallwood Reservoir. We compromised when mines at Shefferville, Wabush, and Labrador City were built. We compromised when non-Innu trappers moved up the Mishta-shipit, Mishikamau-shipu, and other rivers, helping themselves to our hunting and trapping territory, then driving us away from land we had so generously shared with them when they first arrived. We compromised when exclusive harvesting rights to salmon rivers were given to the Hudson's Bay Company and later to private fishing clubs.

These compromises caused starvation and other serious hardships for my people. In fact, there are people alive today who remember what it was like to starve, what it was like to undergo tremendous hardships that resulted largely from contacts with Europeans. They suffered new diseases and watched their land be swallowed up. We are tired of compromises. Our backs are up against the wall. We have nowhere else to go.

Forty years ago we were like someone standing in the middle of a field. You could push that person, he'd move a bit, but it wasn't the end of the world. Today we are like someone standing at the edge of a cliff. To push someone standing in the middle of a field is one thing, but to push someone standing on the edge of a cliff is another matter altogether.

We are, I fear, on the brink of collapse as a distinct people. Like indigenous peoples all around the world, our distinct culture and economy are being crushed by an incredibly greedy and environmentally irresponsible industrial order.

Unless the Canadian, Quebec, and Newfoundland governments change their policies toward us, we will fall off the cliff. We will fall into a downward spin of alcohol abuse, family violence, despair, and other symptoms of cultural collapse.

This is a depressing forecast, and we will try not to let it get us down. We know that it is very important to keep hoping for a better world, for a better relationship with the industrial society that so eagerly grasps our land and its resources.

As you know, we have not been sitting back passively and watching this happen. We have been fighting back with everything we've got. We have made this great sacrifice by going to jail far away from loved ones. It has been emotionally draining and stressful for us, but it also strengthened our resolve to keep fighting to proctect our way of life and our rights in Nitassinan. We and other indigenous peoples around the world need to stand together in opposing militarization and all other devastating changes that industrial countries are imposing on us. But we will need the support of others, particularly of the newcomers who came to our lands and may not have been aware of the harm their governments have caused us.

Recently we have entered into land-rights negotiations with Canadian governments, but many of my people have a deep mistrust of the whole land-claims process. They feel it is a real estate deal where they lose their land and rights for money. I sincerely hope they are wrong. We are not at all interested in this kind of settlement. We want a fair settlement for the Innu nation as a whole. This is where other people can make a difference, too. I hope many people will come to know us better and understand the plight we face. We have fought with dignity and ingenuity, but our struggle isn't over yet.

RIGOBERTO QUEME CHAY

(Maya/Guatemala)

The Corn Men Have Not Forgotten Their Ancient Gods

The Mayan civilization took root in the Mesoamerican region, and its descendants now live as far south as Guatemala, southern Mexico, and parts of Honduras. Today most of them can be found in Guatemala, where 5 of the country's 9 million inhabitants form part of the Mayan civilization, a mosaic made up of twenty-two ethnic groups speaking as many different dialects. The most numerous groups are the Mame, Cakchiquel, Kekchi, and Quiche. The author of this essay, Rigoberto Queme Chay, a researcher and communal leader, belongs to the Quiche group.

The Mayan culture, still alive today, has managed to survive five hundred years of colonization, a process that started with the conquistadores and continued at the hands of their descendants. Over all these years, we have been on the receiving end of a constant offensive against our forms of production and social organization, our culture and our religion, in reality a cult of nature.

We Mayas have invented forms of resistance to conserve our values. In some cases, this has enabled us to reject the values of the invaders, in others to adapt them, and in still others to accept them.

Rigoberto Queme Chay (Maya/Guatemala)

The Guatemala of today is a country torn by serious social conflicts rooted in two very different forms of life, two cultures tied together by a bond of domination-subordination. The aim of the conquistadores was to introduce Christianity as a form of ideological control and justification for new forms of oppression and exploitation of both man and nature.

As far as religion is concerned, the "cosmovision" of the Mayas differs fundamentally from the Jewish-Christian ideology forced on us from 1492 onward. The essence of the globalizing character of the Mayan religion lies in the way man sees himself and his relation to the world that surrounds him.

In the first place, time and space for the Mayas are primogenital gods, and nature is the superior force from which emanates the authority that gives direction to life and to the reproduction of all beings. Mayas believe that all nature is life: each animal, stone, and river has its own *nahual* or "divine personification."

The earth and water are superior to all other elements of nature because they are the origins of life. "Thus, for example, Tlaloc (in Nahuatl) or Chaks (in Yucateca Mayan) are the guardian gods of the rain, who pay particular attention to the milpas (the areas of land dedicated to corn growing) where tribute is paid to them, their intervention sought to ensure good harvests, and thanks given when that happens."*

Man bends to the design of nature, which he does not consider alien to himself and which he cannot exploit without mercy. The irrational use of the natural resources made available to man is held to be a sin.

A Mayan year is divided into 260 days, further divided into thirteen

---

* *Carlos Guzman Bockler,* Donde Enmudecen las Conciencias *(Where the Consciences Are Silent), (Mexico City: Secretaria de Educación Pública, 1986).*

months, representing the cycle of corn in the bowels of the earth and the gestation cycle of the human being in the womb. Tradition has it that man was made from the dough of yellow corn after many attempts by his creators. Corn is omnipresent in all human activity, as food, as decoration, and as religious symbol. Most meals are based on corn, which, with beans and chili, makes up the basic diet. The dominant colors in women's clothes are yellow and green, the colors of grain and the leaves of corn, and the designs used for decoration recall the leaves of the plants.

The Mayan farmer observes certain propitiatory rituals and asks forgiveness for the wound he is about to inflict on Mother Earth. This has been the way since time immemorial, as referred to in *Pop Wuj,* * the sacred book of the Quiche-Mayas:

> Oh God, my father, my mother,
> lord of the hills and the valleys,
> spirit of the forest, look after me.
> I will do as I have always done.
> I will make you my offering.
> I want you to know I will hurt your heart,
> but please allow me.
> I am going to stain you,
> destroy your beauty,
> farm you so that I can live.

---

* Pop Wuj *is the correct title of the book that has been widely distributed under the title* Popol Vuh. *The latter is the name that was given to the accounts of the Quiche-Mayas when they were translated into Spanish. The expression* popol *has no significance in the Mayan language, while* pop *is the name given to the grass mats used in homes or ceremonies on which women kneel.* Pop *is made with vegetable fibers that form a crossed web, analogous to thought and understanding, according to the Mayan cosmovision. Thus,* Pop Wuj *means a book of understanding, of science, of wisdom.*

Rigoberto Queme Chay (Maya/Guatemala)

Religion is lived in a very particular manner in Guatemala today. The external manifestations seem to indicate religious syncretism. But deeper observation shows that many of the religious values the Catholic church tried to impose through doctrine and force were only superficially accepted. What happened was that the most ingrained beliefs adapted themselves to new circumstances and generated resistance strategies for their self-preservation. Rightly so, it has been said that "in face of the degree of abstraction of the American cosmogonic religion, Catholicism found itself disarmed, and thus unable to attack [that religion] at its very base."[*]

The most representative ceremony of the Mayas since long before anyone can remember is that which celebrates the first day of the Mayan year, *wajchakib batz*. Thousands and thousands of people take part in the ritual and identify themelves culturally as the heirs of the Great Mayans. Invoking nature and the heart of the skies and the earth, in a world marked by the rapid decay of its natural resources, the millenarian agrarian religious ritual takes place in cave and mountain temples constructed especially for the ceremony, in the interior of the countryside, and even on the outskirts of the major towns.

The event is significant for three major reasons: first, the striking boom in the practice of the ritual, with ever-increasing numbers of people taking part despite opposition from the state and the church (Catholic and Protestant), and its gradual emergence from the clandestinity that surrounded it until just a few years ago. Second, the fact that its celebration has extended to sectors of the population with a certain level of education and socioeconomic status, including academics. This refutes the notion that only the poor and ignorant are practitioners, and it also challenges the definitions of paganism and

---

[*] *Eric S. Thompson,* Historia y Religión de los Mayas *(History and Religion of the Mayas), (Mexico City: Editorial Siglo XXI, 1986).*

fraud that have been applied to the religious celebrations of a large sector of the population. Finally, the fundamental core of the religion consists of the cult of nature and respect for and subordination of man to nature (not the reverse, as happens with the culture imposed by the conquistadores).

The early 1870s saw the introduction of some industry and the exploitation of coffee in Guatemala, and with it the start of the process of capitalist industrialization that has since governed attitudes to nature.

Coffee cultivation requires extensive surface area, and this inevitably led to the abolition of communal ownership of the land. This in turn led to a strengthening of *latifundios* (large estates) where previously *minifundios* (smallholdings) had flourished. The best land ended up in the hands of a few, and the indigenous people were forced to expand their agricultural frontiers using methods that ran counter to their cosmovision, such as the burning of forests and the use of mountains to replace the forests from which they had been expelled. Feudal-type agriculture and the defective process of industrialization constituted the base of an economy that privileged the search for maximum profit and was thus insensitive to nature. The irrational exploitation of natural resources together with the environmental problems caused by urbanization have led to soil decay, air and water pollution, the loss of biodiversity, climatic change, and the inadequate handling of solid waste.

There is a common denominator in all of this: the worst affected have been those whose view of nature and its resources are based on respect. There is a high correlation between deterioration of the living conditions of the Mayas and the deterioration of nature. At the same time, necessity forced peasants into a confrontation with Mother Earth in such a way that both, the Mayas and nature, are today fighting a huge battle for survival.

In the agricultural sector, this process can be seen in the disappearance of vast wooded areas to make way for exploitation of trees and the growing of crops such as cotton, banana, coffee, and cardamom, which need heavy use of chemical fertilizers and insecticides. This has badly affected soil fertility and led to the extinction of animal species. Peasants found themselves forced to plant corn for their own consumption on mountain slopes that are so steep and inaccessible that people say you have to sow with blowpipes and harvest with helicopters.

The use of wood as a source of energy, which is very widespread in Guatemala, is an outstanding example of this situation. Peasants depend on wood not only for cooking but also for obtaining a few cents more to supplement their precarious incomes. The law provides for sanctions against those who are not authorized to fell trees. How strange then that the small farmers are not given permits, while the big companies regularly chop down ten times more than they have been authorized to fell because of the lack of sufficient control. This is how the small tree-fellers find themselves outside the law and subject to financial penalties. Meanwhile, though the cutting down of trees for the survival of peasants is punished, the system accepts the fact that big business chops down woods to supply factories and cities with wood.

Further, Guatemala provides fiscal incentives (such as income tax deductions and other advantages) for reforestation. And this is why the big consortia dedicate themselves to reforestation for industrial objectives. One of the effects has been that municipal authorities have dispossessed numerous indigenous communities of their land and turned it over to big business.

The mountains have been enclosed and denuded of their woods to make way for the planting of trees that can be used by the timber industry, with the result that the communities affected face the problem of where to find wood. In the end, they have to travel long It distances because the timber companies deny them access to the mountains. Given that exploitation permits are granted to big business for up to fifty years, it is impossible to pass judgment on what benefits such a system may offer. What is clear is that peripheral communities are suffering from major changes in their productive activity and now find their very survival threatened.

Another new factor introduced by this type of exploitation is the increased frequency of avalanches, and the death and destruction these bring in their wake. On the high plateaus, most of the people live at the foot of the mountain, so when the rains come they face landslides of mud and stone as a result of erosion caused by the destruction of the woods that had previously acted as barriers to such landslides.

Even the extraction of water to satisfy the needs of industry can cause tragedy. At the beginning of 1991, in the town of Zunil, one of the most traditional homes of the Quiche people, a landslide killed twenty-five persons. The disaster was caused by the explosion of a well drilled by the state geothermal energy company. That's why the people now say: "You can't touch the mountains."

The environmental decay of the cities is linked to industrialization and internal migration patterns. According to some experts, "Environmental decay is not a consequence of human progress, but rather a characteristic of certain models of economic growth that are unsustainable in ecological terms, unequal, and socially unjust."*

This description fits Guatemala like a glove. Industries have developed as a result of highly protectionist measures that have generally led to small-scale dependent enterprises. These can draw on huge cut-price workforces forced out of the former smallholdings. The

---

* *Ana Cristina Castaneda, "El Deterioro del Medio Ambiente Nos Afecta a Todos" (Environmental Decay Affects Us All), in* Siglo XXI *(December 13, 17, 18, 1990), Guatemala.*

migration from countryside to city, as in other Latin American countries, has stimulated a growing but disorderly urbanization that is lacking in minimum social services.

The rate of urbanization has accelerated in recent years because of the economic crisis and the widespread violence that has affected rural dwellers in particular. In most major towns, as well as in the capital, which is home to 25 percent of the entire national population, there has been an upsurge in problems of overcrowding, delinquency, prostitution, unemployment, urban marginalization, and so on. Residential areas apart, all towns experience a shortage of drinking water and drainage systems, together with a lack of housing, electric energy, and health and education services.

The migratory flow toward urban centers has three major sources:

1. Maya farmers who have been left with no land to cultivate, most of them having been displaced by the expansion of *latifundios;*

2. Maya peasants uprooted from their communities to undergo military service and training to bring them in line with what the state deems necessary to maintain the status quo;

3. Mayas who have found themselves unwittingly involved in the civil war between army and guerrilla forces. The Mayas are used indiscriminately as human shields by both sides and as such suffer the direct impact of the institutionalized repression that reigns throughout the country, a system that is inseparable from the colonial process started five hundred years ago.

No statistics exist that can adequately define the scope of the problem. What is clear is that the identity and cosmovision of migratory people are affected, and they adapt themselves to the ideological power of the state. This means their attitude toward the environment and nature will change.

Government officials and politicians portray an attitude of egoism and ethnocentrism that assigns no importance whatsoever to rational use of resources. Nor do they give any consideration to the people who live on the peripheries of the major towns. This explains why refuse, sewage, and industrial waste are shunted out to the rural areas with no concern for the safety and rights of the people.

Chinautla is a small Pokoman town, whose pottery dates back to pre-Spanish times. It is located on the bank of a river that today is used to drain sewage from the capital, just fifteen kilometers away. The town has become practically uninhabitable because of the high level of decay of the soil as a result of river pollution. Houses and parks are collapsing and sinking because the river waters have invaded the land.

Nevertheless, the inhabitants refuse to abandon their homes because of the strong socioreligious ties they have with their land. Mayan custom has it that the umbilical cord of the newly born is buried in the house of the parents in the hope that when the baby reaches adulthood he or she will understand the importance of the home and the dependence on the land. That's why it's not easy to give up one's birthplace, even though the circumstances are anything but positive.

The government is not at all concerned with finding a solution to the problems of the towns situated, like Chinuatla, on the sides of rivers that flow down to the sea. The filthy waters that the towns spew out have polluted the rivers, which is what the population, mostly indigenous people, use for their basic needs.

Many argue that the Mayas are happy living in their current condition of poverty, ignorance, lack of health care, and shortage of land because we carry out our social and productive activities accompanied by ceremonies replete with entertainment, music, color, and movement. We are considered folkloristic and picturesque.

The Mayas always have occasion for ceremony, whether for a burial or a wedding. That gives some people the idea that we accept the way things are. The reality belies such judgments. Our people have struggled without respite for their survival. Our demands for land and our protests against abuses and injustice have been violently suppressed for the last five hundred years.

Our resistance continues at various levels and in various geographic regions. Our claims are part of an alternative social model that envisages a type of economic development that is compatible with the preservation of nature.

The Mayas have been excluded from the running of the state and from the formulation of national policies that can express their point of view. The state does not recognize the customary rights of the Mayas nor our forms of social organization, which still remain in place in the rural communities.

We believe that any proposal aimed at finding a solution to the problems of the environment must recognize changes in land ownership patterns. The most important is to preserve and revitalize what remains of the indigenous communal ownership, which the state wants to do away with so that it can throw what little land still remains onto the market.

At the same time, the problem of poverty affecting 80 percent of the population has to be overcome, and there has to be a decentralization to combat the constant centralization of power, services, and investments that runs counter to the interests of rural communities.

Strategies and programs for conserving the environment should be less concerned with technology and education and more with effective community participation in their design. Only in this way can we overcome the technocratic point of view that touches only the superficial level and fails to deal with the deep-rooted and fundamental problems.

It is also necessary to reform the national education system and official training programs, because these cover rural communities in only a partial manner. For example, the language of education campaigns is light years away from that of monolingual Mayas, contains messages that are difficult to decodify, and is contrary to our beliefs, interests, and needs. Most training takes place in Spanish, and bilingual educational projects have not been designed for the diversity of dialects that exists in the country. How can one hope to disseminate understanding through the written word if most of the rural population are illiterate? What can a kid from the countryside who speaks only his mother tongue understand when school forces him to learn Spanish, teaches him about sandwiches, videorecorders, sewers, cables, and toilet paper, and describes North American–style houses and blond-haired children?

But what is most important is that everything be rooted in a political context. As long as the Mayas are a demographic majority but a political minority, the longed-for development tied to environmental preservation will not be possible, for the following reasons:

1. Development has to be based on peace, and this can occur only where there is participatory and representative democracy. This is not the case in Guatemala.

2. Socioeconomic problems (among which those of the environment are of importance) are the result of intolerance, exclusion, the excessive desire for profit, and an irrational approach to progress that is not shared by everyone—despite the "frustrated attempts to impose a code and a unique (colonial) political and cultural design on a pluralistic social grouping that, from the moment of its breaking away from the invasion, declared itself in opposition and took refuge inside a culture of resistance."*

---

* *Stefano Varese,* El Rey Despedazado *(The Torn King), quoted in* Utopia y Revolución (Mexico D.F., Editorial Nueva Imagen, 1981).

3. "The logic of capitalist productive and economic organization, as in industrial and productive versions of historic socialism, is accumulation. The logic of ethnic-Indian economies, whether in the form of home or small market production, is anti-accumulation."*

4. To these, add the fact that for the Mayan culture Mother Earth is sacred and man is part of nature, and one can understand why we claim that the complete integration of the Mayas—with all their values and forms of organization—at the level of the state will lay the foundation for a new structure of society that is the precondition for harmonious and environmentally sound development. The Mayas' territorial claims and demands for self-determination should create the national objective of delimiting the space necessary for developing alternatives to the productive processes that hold sway today.

In conclusion, we have to stress that the final word has not yet been said, and we must listen to the indigenous people before it is possible to construct a new society that can resolve the apparent contradiction between economic development and conservation of the environment.

* *Stefano Varese, ibid.*

MARCOS TERENA

(Terena/Brazil)

Sing the Song of the Voice of the Forest

Marcos Terena was born in a small village in Pantanal, in Brazil's Mato Grosso del Sur. He spent his early years there and only discovered the existence of rich and poor when he began studying in Portuguese.

Terena was founder and president of the Union of Indigenous Nations of Brazil, the first movement ever organized at a national level to defend the rights of indigenous people. He is currently coordinator-general of the Intertribal 500 Years of Resistance Committee.

Terena is a civilian pilot for the National Indian Foundation (FUNAI), a governmental organization. This activity has enabled him to establish links with indigenous people throughout the entire country. He works nonstop to disseminate and defend the realities and demands of native communities.

More than four hundred years ago, the words of an old Tupinamba were recorded by Jean de Lery, companion of Villegagnon, the French commander who fought the Portuguese and Dutch for control of the indigenous seas and the conquest of these lands of Pau-Brasil.*

* *Pau-Brasil takes its name from a native tree of Brazil. Today, the pau-brasil tree is extinct in vast areas where, prior to the arrival of the Europeans, it was the most abundant tree species.*

An old Indian once asked me: "Why do you come so far in search of wood to heat yourselves? Don't you have wood on your land?"

I told him we had a lot, but not of the same quality, and that we did not burn it but extracted color tints. I added that in our country there were traders who possessed more cloth, knives, scissors, mirrors, and other merchandise than he could even imagine, and that one of these traders bought the whole of Pau-Brasil with the laden cargoes of many ships.

"Ah," said the savage, "you're telling me tales of marvels . . . but this rich man you're talking about, won't he die?"

Yes, he'll die just like everyone else.

"And when he dies, to whom will he leave all he owns?"

To his sons, if he has any.

"Well," continued the Tupinamba, "I see now that you're all mad. You cross the seas, suffer all sorts of upsets, and work so hard to amass riches that you leave to your sons and those who live on. Don't tell me that the land you feed couldn't also feed you? We have our fathers, mothers, and sons that we love, but we believe that when we die the earth that has nurtured us will also nurture them. That's why we rest easy."

It must surely have been experiences like this that awakened the interest of great writers and philosophers like Montaigne, Erasmus, and Thomas More—experiences of simple people, people considered to be lacking in everything, but masters of that particular wisdom concerning the essential and universal in the human condition: the practice of a way of life that is socially harmonious, egalitarian, and without major conflict.

But the curiosity of philosophers and humanists was not enough to stop what happened throughout the course of the history of Brazil and other areas occupied by the European colonialists: namely, the enslavement and oppression of the indigenous peoples, in some cases to the point of extinction. The 6 million indigenous people who originally inhabited this country were decimated to the 240,000 of today, a group that would just about fill the Maracana stadium, the world's biggest football stadium.

Nevertheless, five hundred years later, these degraded and impoverished "remains of people" can still teach us much about the rules of living together and about political and social virtues that have practically been forgotten by twentieth-century society, which is breaking up in wars between brothers and in conflicts of extreme violence.

In Brazil there exists the miracle of the Xinguana culture. Despite the linguistic diversity of its seventeen peoples, who still live in their traditional habitats—an ecological oasis in the heart of the central region—the Xinguana manage to promote integrative cultural forms through group activities, such as *kuarup* and *moitara*. The first is a ritual involving barter, the second the definition of jurisdiction through intertribal struggle; both practices substitute ceremonial exchange and sporting competition for conflict.

The indigenous people have been called "the great silent people of history." It is rare for their personal testimonies to reach the Western world. Colonialism and the sinful catechism imposed on their cultures silenced them and ensured that what has been recorded is the poor, summary, and deformed history that a certain viscount of Araguaia described as "the story of the conqueror."

Today, the silence forced upon us has been broken by the words of indigenous leaders and legislators, even though the most eloquent and authoritative of them have been violently silenced, as happened to Angelo Kretan, Marcal Tupa-i, and Hibes Wassu, all three assassinated in the fight for repossession of the lands of their people.

Kretan was the cacique (prince) and political leader of the Kaingang people who live in the south of Brazil. Marcal, chief and leader of his people, was one of the brains behind Brazil's Union of Indigenous Nations and was a Guarani, a people that live on the border between Brazil and Paraguay. It was Marcal who, in 1980, was the Brazilian Indian who met with Pope John Paul II, and on that occasion predicted his own murder. Hibes, political leader of the Wassu people and cofounder of the Union of Indigenous Nations, was assassinated in 1991 by swordsmen wearing the uniform of the Alagoas state police, on the northeast coastline of Brazil. For this reason, it is necessary to listen to those leaders who have been lucky enough to survive.

Not long ago, a Terena chief came to visit us in the Brazilian capital, his first visit to a major urban center. We had hardly set foot on the street before we realized he had no money, so we accompanied him to an "electronic bank" to show him the technology of the white man and his money box. Much to our surprise, when we opened the door of the cabin, we found a poor and unkempt six-or seven-year-old child. He didn't say anything, but his sleepy eyes seemed to ask forgiveness for having been found not in his house but in the house of money.

Several hours later, the indigenous chief asked for further explanation, almost as if he couldn't believe what he had seen. Then he said: "I don't advise anyone to enter the mind of civilized man. He has television, telephones, cars, and huge buildings, but he is unable to feed and house his children. We come from the villages and we don't have this sort of richness. We hunt, fish, plant, and protect our habitat, and children have always been at the center of our attention. When our children come into this world, our people are reborn. When this is no longer possible, we will have reached the end. The day the white man reached our village, we talked and he gave us many gifts to drag us into a new form of civilization. But it was all false, because here we don't live off gifts. That's why I often find myself asking: What does being civilized mean? What does being rich mean? What does being developed mean?"

The schoolbooks used to teach children the history of the "heroic" domestication of the savage Brazilians recount that a certain Portuguese adventurer, when he found that the Indians showed no interest in gold mines and money, and were even less interested in showing them to the invaders, decided one day to issue an ultimatum. He poured *aguardiente* (a whiskylike liquor) into a container in front of the entire village and set fire to it. The "water" apparently began to burn. Frightened, the Indians immediately indicated the site of the mines; for them, the most important thing was to preserve water, which slaked thirst, and not collect nuggets that were completely useless except for driving the whites crazy.

Sometimes we indigenous people ask ourselves: What path does the white man want to follow?

Due to a strange coincidence, today, exactly five hundred years after the first meeting between Amerindian and Western civilizations—who knows if it is not one of the last alarm bells?—the colonizer finds himself at a crossroads: he can't continue turning a blind eye to the high levels of destruction of nature and squandering of raw materials that modernity and advanced technology pull along in their wake. What is in play now is not the enrichment of people, but the very survival of Earth and man. The major unknown factor is how to establish preservation in a world in which technological realities have laid daily siege to the lives of people, even inside their own homes.

In June 1992, Brazil will be invaded by illustrious observers, theoreticians, and environmental experts, almost all of them from the First World. Under the sponsorship of the United Nations, they will gather to celebrate the World Conference on Environment and Development.

Our view is that what we will be facing is yet another demonstration of the economic power of some countries. The nations of the Third World will find themselves forced into humiliating pleas for clemency, almost begging for a handful of dollars that some believe can pull them out of poverty. But what will really happen is a repetition of the well-worn dominating tactic of the rich countries: the perpetuation of economic dependence.

The indigenous peoples have been witnesses to the coming and going of the "civilized" peoples, but now that the United Nations is debating the question of self-sustainable development, we can no longer remain silent. It does not matter how many technical experts exist today who can formulate these and other ideas—self-sustainable development has been the core of our way of life for more than five hundred years. That is why we ask to speak, but not only to speak—to be listened to.

We take seriously current world concern over what we have always warned about. For a long time now, we have recognized the destructive path created by an avaricious process of civilization; we know that it's not a question of visions or predictions, but of a truth that is now being affirmed. The world needs new ways of living.

After having laid waste to the Earth—its soil, waters, and underground—technological man is now looking to the skies and the stars, upsetting the balance of the cosmos by constructing huge platforms of war in the name of peace.

For centuries, even before the Europeans began their search for new conquests, indigenous man has interpreted the signs of the times in the belief that the Earth sustains us like a mother's milk, and our life on it continues in a perfect circle between man, environment, and the cosmos. Indigenous man has been able to decipher the greatness of nature and set down a code of life "civilized" man could never understand, whether in its materialistic or spiritual aspects.

Indigenous peoples have carried this understanding down through the generations from parent to child. But the arrival of a new civilization forced us to change our behavior, to adopt new clothes, new eating habits, and new religions. It was only later that we discovered this was a civilization that had fractured internally, because it had pushed to one side the very structure of natural man, of his spirit, of his soul.

White man's civilization also forced our people to adopt commercial, economic, and social values that we knew nothing about, like the difference between richness and poverty. Later, we discovered how deceitful and despicable these new ideas were, because the end result was social misery and degradation: the development forced on us benefited the few at the expense of the many.

The facades of the beautiful cities hide immense industries that spew out toxic gases and progressively render the air ever more unbreathable. Harmful residues are destroying the rivers and the seas, making water undrinkable for people, birds, and animals. I remember the day we went to visit Brazil's most polluted city, located in the country's richest state. Even though it was daytime, when we looked up to the sky, it seemed like night. Bit by bit, fire and smoke had blotted out the blue sky.

For us of the family of indigenous people, development is not just materialistic, it is also spiritual. We always try to walk the narrow line between the material and the spiritual. We have tried, even when faced with the threat of death, to teach nonindigenous man all of this, because this is something he has to learn. He has to recover this type of equilibrium to become more a person and less a machine. Modern man runs the risk of discovering this when it is already too late, when all that remains is the desert of his illusions; he needs to rediscover a nature that was created to distribute well-being, not to transform that nature into a mere source of profit, not to swap the green of the forests for the green of the dollar.

For five centuries, "civilizing" man has stubbornly refused to understand or respect our philosophy. From time to time, a few thought our ideas were quite nice, but only as poetry, not as a way of life; on other occasions, our ideas were held to be unrealistic or utopian. In fact, what we were saying was obvious, as natural as life itself, and understandable even by children. It is not a simplistic question of proposing an alternative but a question of practical examples, so that our offspring don't forget these truths during their lifetimes and can transmit them, one day, to their offspring.

One day a student came to our village, a future expert and "Indian specialist." He had come to study and analyze indigenous behavior as part of his university thesis. The following morning he was invited by an ancient warrior to visit some other villages, a day's travel away. After half a day of walking, the two decided to take a rest in a quiet place. The curiosity of the young man spurred him into looking around, and at a certain point he found himself in front of a tapir. With a hunter's instinct, he readied his rifle and took aim. As he was about to fire, the ancient warrior stopped him with the following words: "Why do you want to kill the tapir? Are you hungry? What harm has it done you?" The Indian went on: "Maybe you never learned this in school, but we believe that everything that lives in the forest could one day be useful for our survival. For example, tomorrow, when we're hungry or want to invite another village to a feast, we will know where to look. The forest is our supplier of food and construction materials. The forest is also our spiritual temple; this is where we render homage to the great *itu-ko-òviti*, he who made everything."

Today there is serious concern about the survival of Planet Earth. The fears are grounded in scientific findings that man is destroying his own ark of survival, and in particular the Amazon, a natural reserve of immense mineral, food, and water resources, a sanctuary of biodiversity. It is in this region that megaeconomic projects are being constructed that pay no attention to the harmful impact they will have on the ecosystem.

Right in the heart of the Amazonian forest lived a people who did not even know the white man existed—until the day they saw the huge machines march forward, destroying trees, killing animals . . . development had arrived.

From the first moment of contact, the indigenous people have had to accept change, even in their own villages. Later, they agreed to move, in return for promises that their living conditions would improve, but they soon found that wherever they went, groups of nonindigenous people had already been displaced by the *latifundistas* (estate owners) in search of places to settle.

Today the Parakana resist, but it is probable that as each sun goes down they are thinking about the distant lake that now stands in the place that was once the center of their history and traditions. There rises the huge hydroelectric plant of Tucurui, which has not only flooded the land of the indigenous people but has also led to the loss of various biological and wood species of the region.

The same happened to the Paratintins, thanks to the trans-Amazonian highway, and to the Nambiquaras, as a result of the BR-364 highway—arrogant progress that generates a form of development that impoverishes and degrades the natural habitat of men, animals, and plants.

The entire Amazon region has seen the construction of highways, hydroelectric centers, and plantations in the name of a concept of development that is largely financed by the government and multinational institutions like the World Bank and the Inter-American Development Bank.

The indigenous people, the first victims of these projects, have always tried to live in harmony with Mother Earth. We don't think of ourselves as preservationists but rather as people born with the values of self-sustainability. We read the warning signs that nature emits, signs like climatic change, the taste of the waters, and the sad song of the birds.

In our village meetings, we have thought much about the white man's way of life. Even though they call us "savages," we have always been convinced that, one day, the white man would hear the messages of nature. That day has come; it's enough that the machine called "satellite" takes photographs of the harsh reality to ensure that our centuries-old call be fully understood.

This has made us think of the arrival of the white man on our soil, with his strange languages and customs, promising a better world, a "civilized" world. To show us his ways, he confused us with gifts and practices we didn't understand, like religion, convincing us to hand over the best of what we had, like our houses, our food, our beds.

But one day we realized that behind this apparent friendship lay big interests, greed for gold, money, wood, even if this meant the destruction of that friendship, of our families, of our land. When we finally realized what was happening, it was already too late, because they were already throwing us out of our homes, hunting us down, and persecuting us like bandits.

Slowly, we had to learn the language and realities of the "civilized," and we came to see it was all fraudulent and false, it was all illusion.

When we tried to flee, we didn't know where to go to avoid dying from illnesses previously unknown to us. Progress had to be served, even if the price was burying peoples, cultures, and beliefs, as we saw in the most recent war in Arab fields.

What is the world of the white man? What's happening in his villages? Why, despite so much technology, is the world sick, hungry, and suffering? Why does nobody pay any attention?

Five centuries have forced a harsh silence on us. Now is the moment to break that silence. We can no longer remain dumb. The big powers talk of industrial development and richness. But it is a richness that brings with it poverty and hunger, increases social marginalization, and division between brotherly peoples.

We Indians consider ourselves citizens of the forests. That is why we have fought so hard to protect our environment and to obtain a government decree that provides official recognition for our territory. If we achieve this, we can guarantee the survival of our villages and families, but, at the same time, we will be preserving an environment that will have beneficial effects on those who live in the cities.

We hope that with the celebration of the UN Conference on Environment and Development* and the arrival of 1993, the International Year of the Indian, we can shout our hope for life to the whole world.

Indigenous and nonindigenous people must overcome the distances that separate them—economic and social differences, prejudice, ignorance, disinformation—and together they must start writing a new

---

* *We will take part in the UNCED with our own cultural and handcrafted products. Among other things, we will use indigenous technology to construct a village in a wood close to the conference center. Shamans will preach and bless the village, the conference, and the Earth. We will hold our meetings in the village and whoever wants to can come and visit us to learn more about our technology and customs.*

page in the history of humanity. To those who criticize this view as a contradiction of our principles and values, our answer is a lesson that nature itself offers. In the Amazon region, there are two huge rivers: one is black, the other is red-brown. The two rivers meet and for many kilometers run together without mixing, keeping their own colors. They eventually mix to form the enormous Amazon River. In the same way, indigenous and nonindigenous peoples have followed our own paths.

Despite all the massacres (physical, spiritual, and cultural), we resist. And we will continue to keep alive the teachings of our fathers. Rational management of the environment and cohabitation with nature form part of the ancient wisdom of our people. That's why, in the past, we were rich. Thanks to our deep understanding of nature, our forefathers were able to produce a medicine with no side effects and no commercial value, healthy food, and architectural and engineering forms adapted to the forests. We are reliving the dreams of our prophets, and we firmly believe that one day AIDS, cancer, and simple allergies will be cured using plants that come from our land.

The new model that humanity needs cannot be a mere reformulation of the model that was imposed on us by "civilization." Some time ago, we visited a number of countries renowned for their high level of development. Initially, we had the illusion of understanding how a First World country lives. But we quickly found out that even there the people walk a tightrope between dissatisfaction and dependence. They are countries with a thirst for pure water, for unpolluted air, they don't have hunger, but they need a new formula for living.

A cacique who doesn't look after his village will never be a good cacique. And soon he will no longer be the cacique, because he will have been replaced or his village will have disappeared. The caciques of the white man (presidents, kings, mayors) must now, more than ever before, fight to ensure the well-being of their people and to avoid the ecological catastrophe that threatens the common habitat of our huge village.

In the enormous modern urban centers, this will not be difficult to achieve if a start is made with children and the education system. Besides mathematics, physics, and chemistry, it is necessary to educate people about the environment, using ecology as a subject of basic training. Society as a whole must commit itself to the battle to preserve nature—in other words, its very future. Artists, singers, actors, and intellectuals must learn to use their *bordunas* (arms) as weapons of war in defense of life.

We indigenous people have been the guardians of Mother Earth until now. We don't want the march of progress and economic ambition to inflict further wounds. On the contrary, we want to find new allies, allies for the survival of our planet.

Our hope is to reach the four corners of the world with our concerns. Why divide the world into rich and poor countries, into First and Third World countries? In the words of the ancient Tupinamba: "This rich man you're talking about, won't he die?"

When we see a country that dominates, and wants to dominate even more, through its technology, its supersonic airplanes, tanks, and computerized weaponry, we ask ourselves: What is the use of all of this? To invade, conquer, and terrorize other peoples? To violate the sovereignty of others in the name of "national interest"?

When we, indigenous and nonindigenous peoples alike, can look at ourselves without prejudice even though we have our differences, then the medicine of indigenous people will no longer seem evil or magic, and our culture and art will no longer be seen as mere folklore.

Just as we know that we are born and will die on this Earth, we are also sure that the dreams of our prophets will come to fruition and that we will achieve balance on our planet, because man and nature were made one for the other.

When that day arrives, the Indian will once again be rich, together with his ally of tomorrow, the white man. It is only then that we can speak of real development, redeeming a sin and social debt that has lasted five hundred years. Future generations will build on that, leaving behind centuries of violence, destruction, and fear.

And then, once again . . . we will be people.

SALVADOR PALOMINO

(Quechua/Peru)

Three Times, Three Spaces in Cosmos Quechua

Salvador Palomino is an anthropologist, researcher, and journalist who teaches the Quechua language and Andean culture at the Catholic University of Lima. He was alternate general coordinator of the Indian Council of South America (CISA) and founder and director of the CISA review Pueblo Indo *(Indian People).*

In the words of Palomino, the members of the Quechua Nation are "those who speak the [Quechua] language, which the Incas called Runa Simi (the language of the human being). An estimated 15 to 20 million South Americans speak Quechua, even if some linguistic experts put the figure at a mere 9 million. Fifty percent of Quechua-speakers, whether monolingual or bilingual, live in Peru.

"The great Quechua Nation comprises various nationalities and peoples. I, for example, am Puqra. My community is Tinte, a small village of two hundred scattered houses at the foot of Tayta Urqu (Sacred Hill) Santa Trinidad, in the district of Tambillo, province of Ayacucho. The insults of guerrillas and army soldiers has led to the migration of most of the inhabitants of Tinte."

For us Quechua people, religion is really a way of life, a knowing, an understanding, living side by side with the forces of nature in holy mutual harmony. We Indians deify all nature's forces, not because we're afraid or because we see them as something supernatural, but because we have known and understood the truth of their laws. We treat them with respect and recognize the benefits of life that we receive from them. Religion in itself, and all the rites we use to worship the holy Pacha Mama (Mother Earth), are expressions of a mutual relationship between man and the cosmos. That is why today's environmental crisis is for our people a social and historical crisis. We indigenous people only want to live in communion with nature. Any violation of its laws and physical integrity is also an act of violence against our societies and our people themselves.

All the world's peoples have their roots in one natural and common spirit. It is we Indians who are today's guardians of this spirit, a spirit that shapes an entire system of life, in spite of the insurgence and domination of the Western system, which, to our eyes, is antinature and egoistic.

In the Quechua language, the words "religion" and "god" do not exist, but we use them in Spanish to indicate our relationship with the divine beings that are the holy forces of nature.

In the enormous and harmoniously balanced family that is the cosmos, Tayta Inti (Sun) is our father and Mama Killa (Moon) our mother. This is what we have learned through an ancient song that goes, "The sun is my father, the moon is my mother, and the stars are my brothers." We worship Tayta Inti because without its rays there would be no life in this world; in the same way, Pacha Mama is Mother Earth; Amaru is the river, the water of life; Wiraqucha and Pachakamaq are the forces that regulate the universe; and Wamani, Illa, and Mallku Kuntur are the messenger spirits, the visible signs of man's communion with the infinite cosmos.

According to our people's concepts of space, Uku Pacha refers to the bowels of the Earth; Kay Pacha is the world of here, of our present life; and Hanaq Pacha is the world above us, the space that surrounds Mother Earth.

In our mythical way of thinking, there exist beings that unite and intertwine these three worlds: Yaku Mama, the mother of water, and Sacha Mama, the mother of the trees. These holy beings take the form of serpents and cross the three worlds: they emerge from the inner world, cross the world of the water, and reach Hanaq Pacha, where they are transformed into the ray, Illapa, and the rainbow, Chirapa, before returning to Kay Pacha and Uku Pacha to fertilize and give color to the plants and all beings. (This belief has been coherently written down by our wise man Hatun Amawta, Luis Valcarcel.)

The three times and the three spaces are part of the same whole unity and are fused together in the cosmos, where life and evolution flow in everchanging cyclical spirals.

For the Quechua "cosmovision," unity is the couple, not the individual. This is a belief that sums up in one practical expression the laws of nature. We believe that the dual, horizontal, and complementary relationship always generates collective and communitarian organizations. This is the concept that gives rise to the Indian institution that can be expressed in the words "mutual harmony" and that in its various forms we refer to as *ayni, minka, mita, challay, saminchay.* These are all manifestations of *tinku*, translatable as "the dialectic of the complementarity of opposites."

For us Quechuas, *tinku* is the primary law regulating the cosmos and endowing it with harmony. This belief is common to all indigenous cultures and takes the form of the "micro-cosmos" within the "macro-cosmos." Knowledge of this primordial law is at the very heart of our way of thinking. When applied to the organization of peoples, the principles of *tinku* turn into social forms that can only be collective and communitarian.

The Western system has done the complete contrary; it has converted the law of complementary opposites into the antagonistic "struggle of opposites." It is this way of thinking that has given rise to the class society, whose elites are conquerors and oppressors and where the values propagated are those of individualism, anthropocentrism, and idealism.

Let's take two concrete examples of the application of *tinku*. If I start building my house today, all my relatives and friends, and all the members of my community, will come to help me, not only with their physical labor but with tools, materials, and even with music and dancing and singing. When the occasion arises in the future, I will offer the same level of help, in an act of reciprocity between individuals and families known as *ayni*. Not helping with reciprocal actions generates inequality and the accumulation of benefits in a one-way direction. This is what happens in class-based and economically exploitative societies. Indians will never abandon *ayni* unless forced into submission, which is precisely what happened when the Western model was imposed on the indigenous peoples of America.

Mita is the joint work of nations toward Tawantinsuyu, the grand confederate, plurinational, pluricultural, multilingual, collective, and communitarian state that took shape in the pre-Columbian era and that had as its center Cusco—the enormous road network that covered practically the entire Andes, the thousands of temples and forts, the maximum expression of agriculture with its innumerable artificial terraces, channels, and waterways, which were all the work of peoples who identified with Tawantinsuyu and its forms of organization.

To ensure the highest quality of life for all its inhabitants, Tawantinsuyu arranged its view of the world, its science, its technology, and its social and political organization to meet the needs of agrarian production and productivity. It developed and institutionalized the following practices to strengthen its unique agrarian system:

1. All land belonged to the *ayllu* (community), which distributed and redistributed it according to the needs of its members. Nobody owned private property. After marriage, all couples without exception were given their *tupu* of land (the *tupu* was a measure calculated to satisfy the needs of newly formed families). No *tupu* was hereditary; it reverted to the *ayllu* on the death of the beneficiary.

2. Everyone was expected to be first and foremost a farmer, before chief, leader, priest, craftsman, or philosopher. These secondary specializations did not provide means of livelihood, only honor, hierarchy, or status.

3. Ecological differences were known and classified, from the banks of the rivers and the shores of the seas right up to the snow-capped peaks. An almost infinite variety of seeds and products was sought because they were all adapted to the different zones. The tendency was always toward multiplying availability, and statistics show that we once knew 1,080 types of potato and more than 800 varieties of corn.

4. To protect against erosion of the little land that existed in our uneven geography (and at the same time win new land from the hillsides), millions of terraces were constructed, using a form of engineering that profited from the rains, springs, and seepage as well as a system of high-quality and artistically designed canals.

5. The frozen and deserted plateaus were rendered cultivatable by digging an extensive system of trenches (*waru waru*) protected by banks of earth. This protected against flooding and, besides permitting agricultural production, led to the development of fish farming and edible algae cultivation in those areas where water accumulated.

Salvador Palomino (Quechua/Peru)

The crushing of indigenous cultures, the persecution of their religions, and the destruction of their forms of socioeconomic organization have been recurrent themes over the five centuries that began with the arrival of Christopher Columbus in America. The process was started by the conquistadores and carried on, first, by the governments of the colonial period and, today, by the descendants of the conquistadores.

In every single corner of the world where the Western value system was implanted into peoples of different cultures, the change was imposed and consolidated through domination and oppression. On the American continent, this process has been particularly drawn out, effected through a system of ideological-cultural assault against our peoples for almost five hundred years. Colonialism has cut deep into our spirit and our way of being. It has transformed most of our brothers into marginal beings, without identity, their roots forgotten, distressed and ashamed of themselves, dreaming of being "white," or at least of being part of the Western way of life and thinking.

The result of our being a conquered people is that our sociocultural universe has been buried under the theories and concepts of experts who have misinterpreted our value system, either through prejudice, or through a lack of understanding of that which is different, or as a means of imposing an "intelligent decodification" of our culture in line with the demands of the oppressor's culture. Most writings on indigenous religion, for example, are mere reformulations of Christian theology on a different cosmovision, or attempts to present a cultural crossbreed, where what really exists is a collision between two antagonistic and irreconcilable civilizations.

What is unquestionably real is the survival of both cultures, albeit in a relationship of inequality: the Western in a position of domination, the indigenous in the position of the dominated. This conflict is at its most visible in the forms of oppression that have always been our daily bread: yesterday, the destruction of temples, the persecution and slaughtering of priests, the banning of ancestral rituals, the burning of sacred objects; today, much more subtle and deceptive measures. For example, in almost all countries of America, only the Catholic religion is recognized as an official religion, and it is prohibited to use substances we consider sacred, like coca and peyote, which have been declared "narcotic substances."

For us Indians, it seems illogical that through Western thinking idealism, anthropocentrism, individualism, and class inequality are extolled. Only Western religious thinking conceives an invisible world, populated by gods who are themselves invisible, that is over and above the cosmic reality. For us, it seems unthinkable that man—who as the "beloved offspring," the "son of God," is also divine—should be superior to other living beings and do as he pleases with the Earth, regarding Mother Nature as an object of consumption, to be conquered, suppressed, transformed, violated, poisoned to the point of destruction just to satisfy whims and not needs.

❋

In what I have said so far, there are two concepts of the world that are totally different, opposite, and irreconcilable: the Western and the indigenous. This is why the meeting of the two cultures in America could not lead to crossbreeding, as a third way, but only to juxtaposition or symbiosis and, in the end, forms of domination.

Whether for gain or out of ignorance, the Western system distorted the essence and content of our culture and our beliefs. To achieve this, myths were invented or recreated. If they did not call us barbarians, we were identified as primitive. Our religious practices were likened to satanic and pagan rituals, and our communion with the holy cosmos was seen as a pantheistic creed.

The indigenous cosmovision favors knowledge, learning, and science in general, even if the form differs from the Western cosmovision. "Indian scientific knowledge is cohabitation; develop environmental technologies in close ties with this cosmovision," as our Guajiro brother Saul Rivas Rivas put it.

We believe that a conceptual pollution hangs over indigenous culture, history, and ways of life that has caused us serious damage: it has attempted to make us forget our people's collective forms, to lead us toward individualism and a class structure, to distance us from communion with the holy Pacha Mama, while at the same time it has incited us to become its enemies, in the image and likeness of Western behavior. It is easy to overcome and suppress any people that loses its communal roots, its identity, and its personality.

❀

How did the pillage start and how far has it gone? The experts estimate that when the Spaniards arrived, there were between 27 and 30 million inhabitants in Tawantinsuyu, and that despite this very high number, this people had food reserves in the *tampus* for several years.

The Spaniards gave top priority to mineral exploitation, and to achieve their ends they enslaved our people, sending thousands and thousands of indigenous people to the mines. The overwhelming majority died, and the land, uncultivated for many years, fell into decay; the Andes began to crumble and the seeds to disappear. This was the first sacking of nature and the root cause of our first poverty and first hunger.

Socially and economically, our lands and the *ayllus* passed into the hands of the Spaniards. This is a situation that persists even today, with our communities prisoners of the estates owned by the descendants of the Spaniards, the neo-Creoles. The invaders appropriated the best land in the valleys, and the surviving indigenous people were forced to take refuge in the inhospitable highlands.

It was at this point that the division between "Indian food" and "food of Western origin" started. Wheat, barley, peas, chickpeas, and so on extended right up to our fields and became part of the Indian diet. We welcomed them, and today barley soup is a staple favorite of the poorest Indians. But prejudice saw to it that Indian foods, like vegetables we know as *oca, maswa, achita, olluco, quinua, ataqu,* and others, have been kept well away from the Creole dining table. *Achita* and *kiwicha* were banned during the period of Spanish colonialism and persecuted as "food of the devil." We have had to wait until they were used as food for NASA astronauts before they merited the interest of agronomists and state authorities.

With the estates also came the introduction of extensive single-crop farming geared toward the market, a system that started immediately to destroy our indigenous system of multicrop farming in favor of self-consumption. In my community of Tinte, which is in Ayacucho, a normal small farm grows corn combined with *quinua* or *achita, porotos* (kidney beans), *cayhua* (pumpkin), *qawinka,* and *araq-papa,* a potato that nobody cultivates but that is picked twice a year because it always appears alongside the other vegetables.

This system is disappearing because of the introduction of beer barley and the increase in potato production as a result of strong demand from the urban centers. This has led to the use of fertilizers and synthetic compost, and in turn to soil depletion and the appearance of pests that we do not know how to get rid of, not even with the most powerful insecticides, which in turn are increasing the degradation of the Earth.

The abandonment of Andean technology (for the last five hundred years) has contributed to the opening up of rifts and deep gullies on the slopes of the hills. Increasingly, year after year, the heavy rains wash fertile soil downhill from the small farms into the rivers and down to the sea.

But the biggest threat—even if there are some signs of action to defend some Indian agricultural products—is the gradual loss of our natural seeds thanks to the invasion of imported seeds. The disappearance of these seeds would be a disaster: it would force us into the clutches of Western technology, lead to the total Westernization of the Andes, and mark the final systematic insult to the nature of our territory.

We can point to other very serious examples of the deterioration of our environment as a result of the expansion of Western-style "modernity" and "development." Lake Titicaca, the world's highest lake (in Quechua, Titi Qaqa, "Rock of the Cat," and in Aymara, Winaymarca, "The Eternal People"), is the center of creation and life for the Indian peoples. From its waters emerged our ancestors Manco Capac and Mama Ocllo, the founders of our cultures. As explained by our Aymara brother Roberto Aruquipa Amaru, from the community of Choqasiwi on the banks of the great lake, "The lord of Winaymarca is Quta Achachila. He is one of the gods of the lake and is identified as the water. The whole of Lake Titicaca is a god." The waters of Winaymarca fall and rise in rhythm with times of drought and heavy rains. Everything having to do with the cycles of the lake is observed, classified, and passed on to the people by Jilire Quta Qilaqata, Indian priest and wise man, who is our link with Winaymarca. The receding waters of the lake throw up extensive tracts of fertile beds of sediment (*aynuqa*). These are shared among all families of the community by Jilire Quta Qilaqata, who sets aside a part for communal cultivation. The *aynuqa* immediately fill up with temporary shacks, small farms, and animals that feed off the fresh produce of the lake. Jilire Quta Qilaqata establishes the times of the rise and fall of the lake by watching the level of water surrounding Maqawi, a small island in the middle of Winaymarca that is also an altar for the cult of Quta Achachila. The established permanent houses have always been built in the high parts of the hills (*sayanas*), and it is here that people live when the waters cover the banks of the lake.

Nevertheless, all this harmonious cohabitation has entered a phase of slow agony, and it is only in the most isolated areas that the authentic and rich ancestral ways continue. The Jilire Quta Qilaqatas are dying off without having been able to leave any of their knowledge behind, because their offspring, submerged in the culture of Western education, now laugh at the customs of their ancestors. The order managed by these ancestors has given way to the ignorance and disorder of the acculturated Indians and the Creoles who are today surrounding the banks of the lake with Western-style permanent urban dwellings.

Rubbish and waste are poisoning the waters of the lake and destroying fish, birds, edible algae, and all other forms of life. Launches and motorboats have taken the place of reed canoes to indulge in indiscriminate fishing, while tourism and sporting activities are on the increase.

And, like a curse, the *aynuqa* of many lakeside communities are beginning to turn into sterile salt-filled land. If this process continues, the consequences will be catastrophic for the very existence of our ways of life. Failure to understand this problem and take the necessary steps will signal the disappearance forever of plants rich in protein and vitamins, reeds like *janchallaya* and *oqururo;* fish like the *qarachi* and *suche;* and birds like the *chuqa, achachito, tikitiki,* or *qiwlla.* And a vast number of indigenous people will swell the ranks of the consumers of flour and other products that the good people of Europe or the United States make so desirable and sell at low cost to the poor of the world. This is how we, knowledgeable wise men and regulators of the best ecosystems that we were, will become miserable beggars.

(To cap it all, as I am writing this, it has just been reported that in the area of Lake Titicaca, oil reserves have been discovered . . . We all know the devastating power of all forms of oil exploitation, and many groups of native forest-dwellers can testify to the death-with-no-return that this means for rivers, lakes, woods, and villages in an extensive area.)

And what can we say of the cities? Our criticism of the Western-style city is also rooted in a comparison with our ancestral cities. The Tawantinsuyu was an agrarian-based civilization, where the city only served to function as a religious and ceremonial center, for administrative purposes, and as a marketplace for the exchange of goods.

Under the system of *ayllus,* houses as well as land distribution and production patterns were organized in a different way. Houses and villages rose in the foothills, either to preserve the pampas as agricultural areas or to protect them against natural phenomena. This meant not building houses on the sediment beds thrown up by lakes or along the paths traced by the avalanches as they charge down toward the rivers.

The introduction of the city along Western lines took place around 1570, alongside the introduction of settlements by Viceroy Toledo. Ever since then, cities that pride themselves on being modern and civilized, like Lima, have continued their blind pattern of growth on the floodbeds of rivers—the Rimac and its tributaries in the case of Lima. The almost yearly avalanches and floods that this produces are attributed to the wrath of God or nature. Doesn't such neglect seem incongruous?

❄

Today, we are witnessing the implementation of huge programs (often with foreign aid) that mean one thing for our people, the arrival of acculturation, de-Indianization, and integration into the Western model, which the West claims is the only road toward modernization and development. We don't agree with this model of development because it is precisely this that has led to the current environmental crisis, in Peru and in the world at large. Either we change tack, or we are headed toward a holocaust, destroying Mother Earth and her offspring.

Our questions are: Does modernity only destroy? Wouldn't it be worthwhile learning something from the indigenous ecosystems? On this land of ours, wouldn't it be logical to work together with the natives themselves to develop adequate—and mixed—technology for an agriculture that respects the idiosyncrasy of the peoples of the Andes and the woods, as well as their ancestral knowledge? The answer is yes, and that leads me to outline a number of ideas.

The woods that populate the planet are the lungs of the world. They contain innumerable species of trees and plants that constitute the habitat for thousands of animal life-forms. Within this conglomerate, each single element is indispensable for all the others: the presence of one benefits and facilitates the living conditions of the others, and vice versa.

The wood dwellers have developed an ecosystem based on cohabitation with nature. Their system of agriculture uses seeds that blend in naturally with the forest-based plants. You can hardly even see their agriculture, hidden by the immense beauty of the forests.

What did the West bring to our Andes and our woods? The destruction of diversity and the arrival of single-crop farming. At the end of a number of years, vast areas were desert, poisoned by fertilizers and insecticides, the rivers dead, species extinct, and the Indian people cornered and stripped of the bounty of Mother Nature.

It has been calculated that 65 percent of the foodstuffs used worldwide today come from America. They are a contribution of the genetic engineering developed by our ancestors over thousands of years. Today, for economic reasons, the system of Western exploitation has appropriated a very narrow range of seeds and has replaced food quality with deceit, using artificial processes to give foodstuffs size, color, and shape that tempt consumers to buy them even though they contain little in the way of nutritional value.

In plurinational and pluricultural countries like Peru, where there is a very pure indigenous scientific-technological-cultural tradition, it is absolutely necessary to draw up a development strategy that hands back Indian rights and guarantees the full independent participation of Indian peoples. Only the independent exercise of our science, technology, and resources, in harmony with the positive contributions of the Western system, will enable us to recuperate species and crop variety and to recover the liberty that was wrenched from our peoples.

The Earth, our Mother Earth, has always been part of the collectivity. We belong to her, she does not belong to us. Land and community are the soul of our peoples. Nevertheless, private property has been introduced into our world and is unbalancing, destroying, and alienating us. Collective holdings in the framework of communitarian organization is the system that is in line with the spirit of our peoples.

This model does not run counter to a new form of planned development, and we prefer it over all other forms. Even if the national territories of our peoples have been expropriated and are now immersed in the new frontier-bound nation-states, we should at least respect communal territories and resources.

We make a common call to all indigenous American communities, that we agree on a series of claims. First, we demand that the state and its institutions respect and promote religious, cultural, linguistic, ideological, political, and racial pluralism. We also call for the legal recognition of the indigenous territories and our forms of social organization. In this sense, communal landholding is an integral part of our culture. At the political level, we aspire to autonomy and self-determination in those countries where we are the minority, just as we aspire to form governments with programs inspired by the indigenous model in those countries where we are the majority.

In these territories we will introduce ways of life and production systems that are in line with our values of harmony with Mother Earth. Wherever an indigenous government takes root, nature will be preserved and will regain all its previous richness and splendor. On this basis, we would be able to open up a constant dialogue and exchange of experiences and techniques with those systems dominated by the Western technological model. Here lies the contribution that our indigenous people can make to help solve the universal tragedy that is environmental decay.

Finally, let me make a suggestion that draws its inspiration from our forebears of Tawantinsuyu, who knew of radioactive materials. They called them *aya kachi* (stones or salts of the dead), and they encased them in giant walls. Through the use of myth, all forms of manipulating such materials were forbidden until such time as the mechanisms for handling and using them were known. The insatiable thirst for energy in the West and its consumer society has carried such manipulation to the extreme, but no one knows how to eliminate the radioactive waste spewed out by the nuclear industry. We believe that when it comes to nuclear energy, Western leaders should do what our grandparents did: suspend everything until they are in a position to control all phases of exploitation and elimination of waste with no risk whatsoever for human life and nature.

ALBERTO HOTUS CHAVEZ

(Rapanui/Easter Island)

If You Sell the Earth, What Happens to the Sun?

Easter Island is home to three thousand people: there are a few Chileans married to islanders and a handful of officials from government institutions, but the majority are Rapanui Indians.

The island is currently a province of Chile, with its governor named by the government in Santiago. Nevertheless, the Rapanui have managed to hold on to their ancestral form of self-government, the Council of Elders. In the words of its leader, "The council is the entire island, the sum total of all Easter Island families, wherever they are living."

Members of the council are representatives of the thirty-six Rapanui groups on the island, each of which is composed of several families.

In recent years, the islanders have registered some progress in their long struggle to gain recognition of their culture and their rights. The juridical and political status of the Council of Elders, for example, had long gone unrecognized by the Chilean state, but the government of President Patricio Aylwin has now recognized the council as its interlocutor within the Special Commission for Indigenous Peoples, a ministerial body.

The author of this essay is the president of the Council of Elders, Alberto Hotus Chavez (Teave). Easter Islanders used to have only one name to identify themselves, but they had to add other names and surnames "à la Spanish" when the island fell under the rule of Chile. The maternal grandfather of Alberto Hotus was Teave; he was forced to add the name Andres and transform Teave into its Spanish version—Chavez.

If a constitutional reform is passed recognizing ethnic minorities, the head of the Rapanui council will be able to go back to his maternal name and sign himself as Alberto Hotus Teave.

At the same time, as the Rapanui leader points out here, his people are waiting for the day they can recover their land and aspire to real independence.

The names Easter Island and Rapa Nui, as well as others that are used to refer to our Pacific Ocean island, located 3,600 kilometers to the west of the Chilean port of Caldera, are of recent adoption. The real name is *pito 'ote henua*, which means "end of the Earth."

Although polytheism exists in the island's religious way of thinking, it was the mysterious Make-make that was considered the supreme creator and regulator of a number of important forces: *mana*, the power of divine beings, kings, and a chosen few; *tapu*, which characterized something or someone that was sacred, inviolable, or prohibited; and *po*, the night, a synonym for the shadows and sleep.

Just like our indigenous cousins in the north of Chile who speak of Pacha Mama or Mama Cunza, or like the Mapuches' Nuque Mapu, we have our own cult of Mother Earth. But maybe it's something rather more profound for us. Our *kainga i'he nue* is Mother Earth, but it also refers to the womb and the placenta. We are sons of the Earth, begot by Make-make, by God.

Tradition has it that Make-make, the supreme creator, fertilized the red clayey earth and gave birth to man. Then, while the man was sleeping, Make-make fertilized the ribs on his left side and created woman. The similarity with the Book of Genesis is clear, and the explanation is simple: the missionary influence on traditional story-telling.

In Rapanui culture, respect for the Earth, the plants, and the eco-system is directly linked with man. Man is nothing if there are no plants, no winds, no water. Man needs all these elements provided by Mother Earth just to live, and that is why the Earth is seen as some-thing given by the god to all men.

When people of Western cultures say the Earth can be sold, we Rapanuis don't understand this sort of language. If you sell the Earth, what happens to the sun, to the wind, to all that is part of nature and inseparable from the Earth?

In our "cosmovision," man must relate to and harmonize with the Earth and nature, making rational use of all that they offer, because the trees, plants, water, and stones are our brothers, are part of man himself.

For the Westerner, the Earth is something that can be given away, sold, pawned, mortgaged. Not for us. We can't touch the Earth, be-cause it doesn't belong to us. It is the property of the gods who have given it to us. We Easter Islanders say: "How generous is this Earth because when one of us dies that person is gathered up in the womb of the Earth."

As far as the religious aspect is concerned, man was seen as incon-sequential before his creator, "a flea or insect crawling on the ground," whose life was fragile and weak, like "a chicken stolen by a man or woman," a simile used to refer to the ephemeral existence of the human being on Earth—the chicken stolen to be eaten straight away.

The spirits that looked after the *tapu* enjoyed happiness in the great beyond. They did not stay with their hungry and thirsty corpses. Our Rapanui ancestors believed in the immortality of the spirit, even if it was impossible to point to any sign of transmigration or reincarnation of the spirits.

Our ancestors also believed in the *akuaku*, the spirits of the night from another world, who on occasion showed themselves to be kind and careful defenders, on other occasions harsh and vindictive punishers of intruders.

A special importance was reserved for the annual feast of *tangata manu* (birdman), celebrated in honor of Make-make in the ceremonial village of Orongo. The feast began at the start of spring, or the *hora* season (spring-summer), and coincided with the arrival of the *manu tara* bird that lived in Motu Matiro Hiva, the Rapanui name for the islands of Salas and Gomez, situated some three hundred miles to the northeast of Easter Island.

Manu tara referred to two types of marine bird: the ash-colored seagull (*Larus fuscata luctuosa*) and the Easter seagull, or the frigatebird (*Fregata magnifens*). The sacred rituals of Orongo had a secret significance and were an exception in the vast Polynesian ceremonial spectrum. When the chief sun-watcher indicated the exact date, the person chosen as *tangata manu* launched himself from the heights of the cliff to swim toward the island of Motu Nui. Once there, the *hopu* (swimmer) had to wait for the arrival of *manu tara* in a hidden location to take possession of the first sacred egg.

Representations of the egg containing the divine spirit of Make-make appear in rock carvings above the figure of *tangata manu*, whose authority lasted only for one year. The last person to have gained this distinction was Ko Rukunga A Mau A Hotu in 1866 when the missionaries had already arrived on Easter Island.

Singular importance was given to the dead, whose bodies were left exposed to the weather until totally decomposed at the hands of the wind, sun, sea spray, and other natural elements, because in those days birds of prey had not yet been introduced to the Rapanui. When the corpse was nothing more than a skeleton, the Rapanui proceeded to the *tanu* (burial), handing it over to the protection of the *avanga* or *ahu* (burial monument).

The *ahu* were divided into two classes. The first were built in such a way as to accommodate a *moai* or *ahu moai* on top, the others not. The *ahu moai* in their most complete form—the giant *ahu moai* that brought universal fame to Easter Island—were built in the period when megalithic art flourished. Thirty-one examples still stand. An estimated seventy-one examples of less complete forms of the *ahu moai* can also be found.

According to ancestral tradition and the royal family tree, Hotu Matu'a was the first *ariki henua,* the highest title given to the ruler of the island, and came from the island of Hiva to settle on Rapa Nui. Hotu Matu'a had been forced to leave Hiva after a cataclysm, and he brought his people to Rapa Nui after first having sent seven messengers, following the instructions of his wise man, Hau Maka.

The island first came into contact with Westerners in 1722 with the arrival of the Dutchman Jacob Roggeveen, who gave it the name Paasch Eyland, or Easter Island, as it is known today.

Between 1862 and 1863, a Peruvian pirate known as Captain Aguirre enslaved 35 percent of the Rapanui people, breaking a long line of harmony in the existing social order and leaving a traumatic wound that took many years to heal.

With the deportation to Peru by the pirate slavers went also the written culture of the *kohou rongo-rongo* (engraved recital boards), whose *ma'ori kohou rongo-rongo* (masters of the recital boards) perished on Peruvian soil, taking the secrets of their science with them to their graves. Even today, it has not been possible to do more than guess at the mysterious contents of the boards, which were engraved in the *bustrofedon* writing, that is, a line from left to right, followed by a line from right to left, and so on.

In 1864, a French missionary, Eugenio Eyraud, began the evangelization of the inhabitants of the island.

In 1871 and 1872, some four hundred and fifty islanders were forced to flee to the Gambier Islands (a small, arid archipelago in the South Pacific) and to the plantations of a certain John Brander in Tahiti, as a result of the tyrannical rule exercised on Rapa Nui by the French mercenary Jean Baptiste Onesime Dutrou Bornier. Dutrou Bornier, a former captain in the merchant navy, turned profiteer, declaring himself *tavana*, the cruel and despotic governor of the island. It was under Dutrou Bornier that the environmental decay of Easter Island began, largely through the introduction of sheep, which transformed the land into a dunghill, and damaged plants, bushes, and vegetation in general.

On September 9, 1888, a "goodwill agreement" was signed between the Rapanui king, Atamu Te Kena, on behalf of the chiefs or elders of the island, and the Chilean navy captain Policarpo Toro Hurtado, on behalf of his government. Under the terms of the agreement, sovereignty of the island was ceded to Chile, leaving the chiefs or elders with their rights and authority of investiture.

Enrique Merlet, a Valparaiso-based Franco-British trader with a reputation as an exploiter, signed a lease to the island with the Chilean government and, in 1895, ordered the building of a three-meter-high stone defensive wall in Hanga Roa, enclosing the islanders in a sort of "reserve" measuring 100,000 square meters. The islanders were expressly forbidden to move beyond these limits.

Merlet exercised such a reign of tyranny over the islanders that the Holy See was forced to intervene on their behalf. In a final outrage, the successor to Atamu Te Kena, King Rirorokom, was poisoned and died in Valparaiso after having been seen for the last time in the company of a trusted employee of the landlord of the island.

In 1903, Merlet gave up 75 percent of the shares in his company, known as CEDIP (Easter Island Exploration Company), to the British firm of Williamson E. Balfour, which kept the company running for another fifty years.

Environmental ruin continued apace with the introduction of 35,000 sheep, 15,000 oxen and 3,000 horses. Rapa Nui witnessed a marked development of its closed culture for as long as foreign ships and airplanes stayed away. The evidence can be seen in the *moai* and stone carvings. But this gave way to an era of decline. In 1928, with the mass introduction of wool-bearing sheep came a major social problem and new employment. Raising sheep meant work and food, even if it also had a negative impact on the environment because of the erosion of the land. Sheep-raising could hardly improve the soil since the soil of Easter Island is naturally fertile and highly suitable for the low-cost production of avocados, pineapples, cassavas, bananas, coffee, potatoes, and corn, among other crops.

The introduction of wool-and-mutton-producing sheep occurred at the same time as the Chilean government was unable to provide the inhabitants of Rapa Nui with meat. But around 1966, two state bodies—the National Development Corporation (CORFO) and the National Forestry Corporation (CONAF)—took over land management on the island, and CONAF closed wells drilled for livestock that was slowly disappearing.

There is a need to find a regulated form of development for some livestock on the island. Our biggest problem, whether as consumers or producers, is transportation. SASIPA, the CORFO affiliate that services the island, provides beef for the islanders through the slaughter of animals on Rapa Nui itself. But the tourist operators, who offer special cuts, have to bring meat in from Chile.

Predator birds did not end up on the island as a result of migration but were introduced in the years after 1928. They were birds of prey, like the *tiuque* (*Mivalgo chimango chimango*), the prolific sparrow (*Passer domesticus*), and the *diuca* (*Diuca diuca*).

The *tiuque*, a type of small South American falcon, was soon baptized by the islanders as *manutoketoke* (robber bird) because of its bad habits.

When CEDIP arrived, the first thing it did was to sow wheat, but this was mixed with radish seeds, and that plant quickly became a scourge. So sparrows were brought in to eat up the radish seeds, and they multiplied so profusely that now there are thousands and thousands of them.

Later, when the same company introduced wool-bearing sheep, the ewes became carriers of worms, so *tiuques* were brought in to feed on the worms and the carcasses of dead animals. This was successful, but once there were no more worms or carcasses to eat, the *tiuques* began to emigrate to the islands of Motu Nui and other nearby islands where the seabirds nested, and so began their extermination, as the seabird eggs were eaten by sparrows.

As far as plant life is concerned, "civilization" brought diseases to Rapa Nui that have proven difficult to eradicate, diseases like *maicillo* and *pata de gallina* (crow's feet), which attack the bushes, such as the *lupino* and guava.

Our island is home to around three thousand people. Every year, a further five thousand tourists arrive, staying on average four to seven days each. This is a massive influx given the dimensions of the island.

Easter Island is in the throes of large-scale tourism that is rapidly becoming a source of pollution. The tourists have their picnics, take their walks, leave their rubbish on the beaches, and throw their bottles and plastic and paper containers into the sea. Pollution is on the increase every day, and if the local population is not made fully aware of the problem, the level of waste and discarded rubbish will continue to rise, with wrappings and containers littering the island everywhere, from the urban to the rural areas.

The island lacks speedy waste-disposal systems. On one occasion when we cleaned up the beaches, four six-ton lorries were needed to cart the rubbish away. You can't have a rubbish dump on an island that has been declared a national park.

At the same time, Rapa Nui is very hot and receives very strong sunlight, so that bottles thrown in fields become magnifying lenses that kindle the grass, setting off fires.

Since we are an island, we put up less resistance than other locations to epidemics, which become difficult to get rid of once they have arrived. In the same way, we are very concerned that tourism is becoming a conduit for the circulation of drugs.

Before giving pride of place to tourism as a source of income, we have to first think of the health of our people and the natural and archaeological patrimony of the island. This is why we believe a type of tourism that is selective and cultural could be a source of progress for the people of Rapa Nui.

Tourism has many factors that have a negative impact on the environment: the indiscriminate pillaging of stones and rocks as new caves are opened up, the masses of yachts around the beach of Ana Kena that spew out their waste and bilge water, because there is no machinery on the island for the treatment of waste.

There is also the excessive exploitation of white coral by Easter Islanders who work below the surface of the water around our coastline and sell it as a "souvenir." As the number of tourists increases, this is becoming a serious problem for the survival of other marine species that rely on the coral for protection and a supply of food. This pillage is indiscriminate and has to be stopped now to avoid serious consequences for the environment in the future.

We are waiting for approval of a bill currently up for discussion that would create the Development Corporation of the Rapanui People, a body that would become the legal administrator of our ancestral lands. Otherwise, we will continue in our state of despoilment, just as in the days when the government of Chile registered our land under its name.

In October 1991, Chilean President Patricio Aylwin signed a project for constitutional reform that would recognize the ethnic minorities of Chile, among them the Rapanuis, as well as another proposal for a law regarding the development of forgotten indigenous sectors. Our position is that these proposals must be accompanied by a law that would create the Development Corporation of the Rapanui People. We firmly believe that the issue is not dead, and we continue to fight for the creation of the corporation.

We feel such a body should be run by ten citizens, of whom five should be elected democratically by the Rapanui people, while the other five should be officials, such as the provincial governor, the mayor, the marine governor, and the heads of CONAF and CORFO, without prejudice to the fact that some of these, like the mayor, have also been democratically elected.

Within the new situation that will be created through the constitutional reform recognizing our existence, the inhabitants of Easter Island will continue to press their case. The main point is that land is a communal good and that the corporation we wish to see created will distribute land according to need.

In August 1988, we, the Council of Elders, filed a complaint against the Chilean treasury for illegal seizure of the land of Easter Island. In

1933, the government of the period had invoked Article 590 of the Chilean civil code and had registered our territory under the name of the treasury. This registration was published in *El Heraldo* of Valparaiso to give evidence of its legality. But that newspaper never reached the island, and, even if it had, there were no schools on the island at that time, so no one would have been able to read of the registration of our land. We still believed in the validity of the "goodwill agreement" of September 9, 1888, which stipulated that Chile would exercise sovereignty over the island but not the right to ownership of our land. This was why in 1989, on the hundreth anniversary of that agreement, we filed our complaint against the treasury. That process is still under way.

We hope that with the constitutional recognition of our people, our land will be returned and we will be able to exercise real autonomy so that we can push our demands for defense of the environment and cultural patrimony of Easter Island.

We want a grass-roots program that begins with ourselves, where the people can plan their agricultural and mining activities and put forward their own proposals for tourism and trade, instead of having them imposed on us from above, as has been the case until very recently.

We hope that once this has been approved, we can begin the direct defense of our environment which is our primary objective. We have not forgotten the Latin expression: *Quis opifex praeter naturam*—"What craftsman exists if it is not nature?"

The Saltwater People

Nathan Wate and his brother George are the descendants of a line of chiefs going back forty generations on Solofou, the largest of the man-made chain of islands in the Lau lagoon near the north coast of Malaita, one of the Solomon Islands. Nathan is chief of Solofou and was a former member of the Solomon Island national parliament. The Solomons became independent in 1978.

Our ancestors were coastal dwellers in the Solomon Islands who started building the artificial islands in the shallow Lau lagoon between coast and reef hundreds of years ago. They moved from coast to lagoon because of the malaria mosquitoes and the almost permanent state of war with the head-hunting hill people.

The artificial islands were built on sandbars or exposed stretches of reef by heaping up boulders. It was here that the saltwater people (as opposed to the hill people) built their houses of sago palm leaves and planted coconut palm trees.

The villages were fortified and divided into male and female sections. Sacred places of worship were taboo for women. The skulls of ancestors who always acted as intermediaries between the living people and nature were kept in special houses. The saltwater people of the

Lau lagoon always kept their gardens on the coast of the main island, near rivers that supplied them with drinking water.

Until recently the Lau people were self-sufficient. They caught fish in the lagoon, made boats from trees that grew in their forests, harvested yams, taro, sweet potatoes, and bananas in their gardens, and supplemented their diet with wild pigs and birds that they hunted in the forest. But the arrival of the white traders, missionaries, and colonialists brought many changes to their customs and traditional way of life.

The Lau people feel the old balance of nature has broken down, with a fatal impact on their subsistence economy. Many elders think going back to the old ways is the only way to restore the balance, but no one really knows how to return to the old ways. Many have no explanation for what caused all the changes—they feel confused and frustrated.

Our nature, our environment, was in balance. We caught plenty of fish in the lagoon. In our gardens we had plenty of sweet potatoes, taro, yams, *pana*, bananas, papaws, and green vegetables. In the forest we hunted for wild pigs and birds. We had all we needed.

We worshipped the spirits of our ancestors. We prayed in our customary ways, and many of our rituals were tied to our ancestors and to nature. We prayed before we planted in our gardens. We prayed before we went hunting. We prayed before we went out fishing. And we had a very special relationship with the sharks, which we believed were the spirits of our ancestors. We were never allowed to kill them. We knew them by name. We called them in order to feed them with pigs. We called them when we were in danger out at sea, and they came to our rescue.

Everything was in balance. Our prayers, our rituals, our ancestors, nature. We always felt that if that balance were to break down, everything would change. That's why it was necessary to keep our prayers and rituals intact. Then the Christian white men came, some ninety years ago. From that time on, everything started to change.

We were told that worshipping the spirits of our ancestors was wrong. The white men told us that we should only worship our creator. And only in the way the white men did. We had always known there was a creator, but we did not know him. Our ancestors were related to him. Our ancestors knew about him. And through our ancestors we were related to him. So we had always left it to the spirits of our ancestors to deal with him.

The white men told us different things. We got very confused. We no longer knew what to believe. We found that the white men were very powerful, they possessed so many things we did not have and had never seen or known of before. So we thought, the white man is so powerful and rich, and the white man also knows so much, maybe he is also right about the spirits.

We became scared, because the white men also told us stories about heaven and hell, stories about horrible punishments. It all made us very frightened and confused. We were no longer allowed to do the things we had believed were essential for keeping the balance.

For example: we were headhunters. We kept the skulls of our slain enemies in very special places that were sacred to us. To have enemy skulls made us strong and helped us follow the ways of our ancestors. We needed skulls to offer our ancestors sacrifices that respected the traditional ways. And since our ancestors helped to keep nature in balance, we had to do the things our ancestors wanted us to do.

That was wrong, the white man said. Then our head-hunting practices ceased to exist. But now we think this was the beginning of all the changes and all the problems we face now. Gradually we forgot about our traditional prayers and rituals. The men of our tribes who had special knowledge of magic and ceremonies no longer passed that special knowledge on to younger people, out of fear that the white men would be angry. So young men never learned the ways we had thought were the right ways for generations and generations.

Our beliefs changed, our customs changed, and from that time on nature changed as well. Slowly at first . . . dramatically in the last twenty or thirty years.

Our population started to grow. In the old days many of our children died after birth. We regarded that as the wish of the spirits. The white man brought what he called medical care to our islands, and the children stayed alive. People of our tribes also grow older nowadays, thanks to the knowledge and care of the white man.

Our numbers have grown. But our land has not grown. All our land is fully occupied by gardens and trees. In the old days we always were able to change, make new gardens every few years, so that the old gardens could grow strong and fertile again. We also were able to plant many different crops in the old days: here taro, there sweet potatoes, over there yams. Now we can plant only taro or yams or sweet potatoes, because the pressure on our land has become too great. And if we have to give our gardens a rest, we can't plant anything. Then we have to buy food. But how do we get the money? We can't occupy new land, because the land next to our land belongs to other tribes who have the same problems we have.

When we had enough land, we kept large forests. There we hunted for wild pigs and birds. But we had to cut the forests for gardens. So the wild pigs and the birds are gone.

Our ancestors had plenty of fish here in the lagoon. Snapper, bream, rock cod, mackerel, tuna, bonito, mullet, rabbit fish, parrot fish, wahoo. But now we find fewer and fewer of those fish in our lagoon. We have to go outside the reef to catch them. But we don't have the proper boats or gear to do that. Besides, even outside the reef, fish are becoming scarce.

What is the reason for all this? Have we been overfishing? Has the environment really changed that much? Are there different currents? And if so, how is that possible?

We can't explain it. We know that big fish factories from a number of countries are floating in the Pacific. Sometimes we hear stories about big boats from those countries fishing in our waters. They seem to use methods that are unknown to us. We have never seen them, but we know that they catch a lot of fish. Could it be that they are emptying our waters of fish? We have heard that our government has objected to their fishing. It seems in vain. We are a small country. Who will listen to us?

We have also heard about nuclear bombs exploding in the Pacific. We don't know about that either, but we have heard that those bombs can destroy people and nature. Why are they doing that?

The white man told us about the creator who creates. He told us that killing our enemies for skulls was wrong. He told us about peace. Then why does he make bombs that can destroy everything the creator has created?

We don't know, but we think that the exploding of these nuclear bombs affects our nature. We are witnessing changes in climate, changes in tides, changes in currents. The tides are much higher than they used to be. Is that because of what the white man calls the greenhouse effect? We don't know what that is, but they tell us that the sea is rising, that many islands in the Pacific will disappear. Is that true? Will we also disappear because all our artificial islands, which our ancestors built hundreds of years ago, are just above sea level? We never had tides covering all our coral ground, we always stayed dry, but now sometimes all our houses are standing in water.

But there's also another side: we had always lived with low tides that lasted only one hour or even less. Now it's three, sometimes even four hours. Small and big fish, and shells and seaweed die.

We think that the reef that always protected us has probably been damaged. How could that have happened? We felt safe between reef and coast—that was the reason our ancestors built our artificial islands. Now we don't feel safe anymore. Is that also because of the nuclear bombs in the Pacific?

We even have more cyclones than in the time of our ancestors, and we recall when a huge tidal wave three years ago was caused by an earthquake that destroyed a large part of the reef . . . our ancestors never talked about earthquakes. We have heard that a cyclone destroyed thousands of houses and gardens on the Samoan Islands. It's true we have always had cyclones, we had learned to live with them, but it seems that now they have become more frequent and have a more destructive power than ever before.

Water and fish are very important to us. We are dependent on water and fish. Even more than on yams and sweet potatoes and pigs. We could, if we had to, survive on fish. But if fish are disappearing, what then? You could say, build big canoes and go out into the open sea. Of course, we could build bigger canoes, but we don't have the land on which to grow trees big enough to carve that kind of canoe.

We never go to the big forest, which covers large parts of the main island, because we don't know the people who live there. But we've heard that the big trees are disappearing there. We've heard logging has become big business. But for whom? What will happen when all the trees have gone? We have heard that this will be very bad for nature, bad for the climate, and bad for the people and animals who are living there and are dependent on the forest. Why do they cut the trees? We don't understand that.

So many things that happened to us after the coming of the white man don't make sense to us. We are no longer allowed to live according to our traditional customs. We have had to change our traditional way of worship and life. Instead of getting a better life, we got more problems, problems we had never known before. Less fish, less fruit from the gardens, less timber. We now need the money the white man introduced. Before, we had a subsistence economy, but now we have become very dependent on money to buy extra food, clothes, materials for our houses, to pay for taxes, and to pay school fees.

We could sell fish on the market. But to catch enough fish we have to go out into the open sea, far away from our island. We can only do that in a big boat. We can't make that boat because we do not have the wood. So we have to buy a boat, but we don't have the money.

Now we have schools. We have education. What can we do with that education? Go to the towns and find jobs. But we only find "No Work" written on the doors and windows of the shops and factories. Our young people have forgotten about our traditional ways, and with the new knowledge they learn in school, they can't get work.

They become very dissatisfied, and many of them are doing crazy things. Before long they will be stealing and robbing. Or they will sit idle, waiting for somebody to help them. Why don't we receive education that suits our village life? A carpenter could teach us how to make new things with old and new materials. We could learn how to fish in a more efficient way. We could learn different and better ways to plant and maintain our gardens. We don't learn that. Instead, what we get is "modern" education that makes us even more helpless and lost and confused.

Since the coming of the white man, everything has changed. We no longer know anything about the relation between us and nature. The Christian churches changed us, and our thinking also changed.

We still often act in traditional ways, but the meaning has changed. So many old things are forgotten. The old people knew exactly when to fish, and when not. And they knew when to stop fishing in certain fishing grounds. Why has all that been forgotten?

We think it's because we don't act in line with our traditional ways. We have been overinfluenced by completely different ways of thinking and doing things. Sometimes we think the white men will destroy the world. They spoil the sea, they spoil the forests, they spoil the air and spoil the land. We blame them for that, yes. They don't act carefully to find out what is good and what is bad for people.

Why do they do that? We think the white men want to be the masters of the Earth, they want to be the masters of all material things, and because of that they break the balance of nature. How to make the Earth healthy again? The most important thing is to live in peace. If we all live in peace, everybody will be happy with nature. But we think it's too late. Nature has been spoiled already. The environment is becoming poorer and poorer, and that causes more and more changes.

Can we go back to the old ways? We don't think so. It would be the best thing to do, to follow again the old traditions of nature. But it's too late. You white people should live in peace with each other, so that we all can live in peace. You control the world, but you have done a lot of bad things to the air and the sea, which makes us at the other side of the world suffer.

DAMIEN ARABAGALI
(AS TOLD TO HERBERT PAULZEN)

(Huli/Papua New Guinea)

They Trampled on Our Taboos

Damien Arabagali, a community leader in Toroba, north of Tari on Papua New Guinea, is one of the first generation of modern educated Huli. His grandfather was a Big Man (traditional name for a man of sterling character—a warrior, magician, or orator; still called Big Men they play a significant role in leading the tribes that lack a chief of their own).

Arabagali has written several essays about the changes undergone by his traditional society and has recently completed a book-length manuscript on the relation between the imported Christian religion and the Huli society. Arabagali often acts as mediator in conflicts involving material damage as a result of gold mining and oil and gas exploration.

In the Tari basin in the Southern Highlands Province of Papua New Guinea, in a swampland area surrounded by dramatic lime-stone cliffs and bush-covered mountains, live the Huli people.

The Huli are one of the largest language groups of Papua New Guinea. Before the coming of the first white men, some fifty years ago, there were about 150,000 Huli, divided into numerous tribes and clans. They were linked by many customs and trading relationships. They also had a common form of worship, centered on sacred places. They lived in what they themselves call "a perfect state of harmony" with their environment. Much of the traditional way of life has broken down since contact with the white men in the 1950s and 1960s. The activities of missionaries not only destroyed aspects of the traditional spiritual way of life, but also caused major damage to the natural and cultural environment.

The colonial administration fragmented the Huli "nation" with its new boundaries. The confrontation with the outside world has speeded up since Papua New Guinea's independence in 1975. Now the area is the center of major oil, gas, and gold exploration that is likely to have a serious environmental impact.

The creation of the Earth started with the eruption of a volcano on the sun. Stones were thrown throughout the universe. One of the stones became the Earth. That's what our ancestors told us. Our belief tells us that the trees were created first on Earth. Then the Earth was populated by spirits, and the spirits became human beings. The environment we have lived in since is like a chain. The sun, the stars, the trees, the pigs, the birds, and all other creatures and men are all part of that chain, all interrelated. We all belong to the universe. We are offspring of the sun. We live in a spiritual world.

From the time of our ancestors, we had found complete unity and continuity. That is why nature has always been very much praised in all our traditional ceremonies. Our tribes and clans and families are all linked to other creatures, like eagles, pigs, or trees, or directly to the sun.

In sacred places we worshipped the spirits—in special forests, at special trees, on special lakes. In some places of worship we have found round stones, which we call the eggs of the sun.

No one, except our priests who had special knowledge of the spirits, were allowed to enter the sacred sites. We were not allowed to hunt there, to wander around, cut trees. We used to call these sites our heavens, because certain huge trees were used by our ancestors to go up—they followed the birds that flew in the direction of the opening in the sky.

There was complete harmony with nature in those sacred areas. Each tribe had such a place, and that place was protected by many taboos.

But not only in such places was there harmony. Rules regulated all our relations with our environment. Young trees and fruit trees were never cut. Herbal plants and trees that provided us with medicine were always protected. Certain animals were never killed. Dogs, cats, lizards, and possums were even regarded as brothers. All natural resources, like salt, oil, shining stones, and crystal, had special meanings for us. We used them to trade with our neighboring tribes or to decorate ourselves.

Every area was divided among tribal groups. And every tribal group used the land according to the traditional relationship with nature. Gardens were set apart from the hunting grounds. Only hardwood was used for building our houses. Hardwood and wood from fruit trees and of course from our sacred trees were never used for firewood. There was complete harmony between human beings and animals and nature. Men, birds, and spirits were especially interrelated. The survival of each was dependent on the other. That balance was a guarantee for survival. Continual and numerous ceremonies kept that relationship alive. Men never stood above nature. Each community felt part of the environment. The community sense was very strong. Everybody had his accepted place in that community.

But then the white men came, and the oneness of the community came face to face with an individual approach, which was completely alien to us. The "I" became the central point. The "others" became stepping stones. "I" had to survive, "I" had to be independent, "I" had to decide for "myself." Very soon, the result of all that became clear: we call it greed.

A great confusion fell on our people. Our old men were watching and listening to the first white men very closely. How they ate, how they slept, what they did, and how they did it. The old men remembered the prophecies of our ancestors about the coming of the white men. Our people found the first missionaries very interesting. They gave them pigs to sacrifice. That was what our people always did. Priests had to sacrifice pigs to make the soil rich and fertile, the hunting abundant, and the weather favorable. But these white priests asked: "Why?" They did not accept the sacrifices and told our people that we were no longer allowed to do that.

Soon we were affected by all kinds of illnesses that we had never known before. Fighting broke out—more than we had known traditionally. There was complete confusion and disorientation. Our traditional places of worship were destroyed. The harmony disappeared. Trees that had been protected for centuries by our traditional laws and customs were felled. Sawmills were introduced. Pine trees in our special sacred places were cut to build mission houses. Our sacred places were called evil. Our trees were cut and dragged away, even out of the country, and these trees were never replanted. In this way, the missionaries contributed directly to the destruction of nature. We were also confronted with forced labor to construct roads that went straight through many of our sacred places, through mushroom areas, through hunting grounds, through breeding places of birds, through gardens. Along these roads Western-style buildings were constructed, so more and more timber was used.

New roads and airstrips in remote areas opened up the country, which had been isolated and cut off by tribal boundaries and taboos for generations. This brought together people who had been enemies before. That might have been a good thing, but this development caught us unprepared for the many abrupt changes in social life it brought with it.

Many of the traditional ways of life, especially religious, have broken down since the first contact with the white men in the 1950s and 1960s. The activities of the Christian missionaries not only destroyed aspects of our traditional spiritual way of life, but also caused major damage to the natural and cultural environment. The colonial administration fragmented our people with new district boundaries.

Of all these impacts, the destruction of the sacred places by the missionaries is felt by many of us to have been the most serious. It has led to general outrage. All the magnificent stands of pines and other forest preserves that marked these sites have been cut down and sold to mission sawmills. The white men have taken our timber to build schools and hospitals, but above all to build their own high-quality homes. Of course there have been protests, but the signatures of the leaders of our people on petitions have brought no response from the new provincial government or the missionaries directing these acts.

With the opening up of new areas, new values we did not understand came in. Taboos were trampled on. There was an enormous impact on our traditional system and on the discipline of our youth. There was a rush to the plantations on the coast. There, our people were faced with a whole set of new ideas, and when they came back to our communities they brought these new ideas with them. They returned to their homesteads with a different language and a different authority. The old values became vague. Conflicts, unthinkable before, arose between generations, between those who stuck to custom and those who were influenced by the customs of the white men.

Complete confusion! The elders did not understand all this. Their world changed under their very eyes and they could not stop it. Many were not able to cope with all those changes. The disruption of social life had really started and there was no return.

In traditional society, each person had a special role. Now it became the survival of the fittest instead. I, I, I, me, me, me—"I" can step on everybody to get what "I" want.

People tried to move beyond their limitations. The young felt more attracted by the wealth of the white men: axes, clothes, money. Especially money. Money changed our subsistence economy, and money became the road to all evil. The individualism brought in by the Europeans has not fully taken root yet; there's still a community aspect. But the traditional sharing of wealth is changing rapidly nowadays, especially among the better educated of our people.

The old sense of interrelation, the old traditional way of respect and discipline . . . all that is vanishing. Look what we learn at school now. It's irrelevant. How to become a European!

No longer the sense of belonging to the group. No longer the feeling of going back to the land. The dream of many now is to go abroad, run after money. Get rich fast! Become somebody fast!

But look what is happening all over the country. The educated can't find jobs. They loiter around in towns and cities, frustrated, undisciplined. They become lawbreakers and create a safety problem everywhere, making traveling on our new roads dangerous, making walking about dangerous, which causes the police to shoot our own people, the foreigners to leave, the law-abiding citizens to hide themselves behind barbed wire fences.

It's giving our young nation a bad name in the papers of the world. I think there's still a chance to stop that downward road and stop the destruction of the environment. Bring back discipline. Young people should come again to listen to our tribal leaders. Young people should be taught the traditional ways before going to modern schools. And those schools should be more land-oriented. Our young people should learn at school how to respect our nature, how to plant and protect trees, how to grow vegetables, how to look after drinking places, how to build their own houses, how to be a carpenter, how to be a farmer. Practical lessons. Relevant for rural areas. So there will always be a basis to return to. Education has to return to the land. Education has to be in harmony with the environment.

The system is here, but no longer used. The government does not seem to see that. There should be more cooperation and coordination between government departments like forestry, public works, education. The school system should stop producing losers. Stop telling people: "If you fail, you are rubbish." That is why our old people think that school is a waste of time and money.

The future is in the hands of our present-day leaders. I, a Huli, want to contribute to the future. Now we have reached the turning point. If we find the right breed of leaders now, we might be able to stop the corruption that is standing in the way of real development. If not, our country will be running down the road to ruin. And once started, there will be no way to stop it. Today's situation is like a time-bomb.

But there's still a chance. There are still grounds for hope and optimism. Somehow we have to find an improvement in life along the lines of our own roots and culture. There has to be unity. But we don't have peace now, and while there's no peace in this country we cannot achieve anything.

Unfortunately we don't know how to achieve peace. There's so much confusion, even right within my own group. How can we find the balance between Western and traditional values?

Is the Earth sick? Yes. Our ancestors prophesied that we would see the Earth turn sick. When the *kunai* grass in the swamps dries up.

When we dig gardens where the pine trees used to grow. When the wild pandanus trees disappear. When the birds fly away. When the pigs and the children get smaller. When women have children who no longer look like their fathers. This is happening here. We are heading for a period when this land will say: "I can't produce anymore." Our land has been reused and reused. It can no longer reproduce. "I have had enough," says the Earth.

It looks like now is the beginning of a period of mass starvation. I see it before my eyes. The giant trees are disappearing. That is a sign. Look at our gardens. They are smaller than they used to be when I was young. Before, we could live from our gardens. Now these same gardens don't sustain us anymore. The gardens are worn out. We don't allow the land to refertilize because of the demands of our growing population.

The same with our forests. We need more and more material, for more houses, more roads, more factories. Land and forests don't get rest. And there's no more land to prepare. And because there are fewer and fewer trees, the rain washes the soil away. The time is fast approaching when our gardens will say: "Sorry, my friends, we can't produce anymore."

On our land lie mountains of gold. These mountains used to be covered with forests. Our people went there hunting for birds and wild pigs, and they used to gather nuts and herbs and mushrooms. From the mountains flowed many rivers that provided us with water to drink and water to fish in.

Look at what is happening now, since geologists discovered the hidden wealth of those mountains, and the government and the companies realized what this could mean to them. Mining started, regardless of what those mountains were to us. Greed brought our own people to dig in the ground in search of gold. Trees were cut. Big multinational mining companies brought up huge machines by helicopter and started drilling. Chemicals and other dirt started dripping into the waters of the rivers and into the ground. All kinds of waste are being dumped into the environmental system.

People drink from the water, people wash in the water, polluted water. Soon the pollution will enter their own systems and will stay there for generations to come. Not to mention the impact the mining has on our social life—the disruption of family life, the breakdown of morale, the use of alcohol, the fighting, the prostitution.

Now our people are complaining. There's no compensation for the destruction and damage to vegetation. All those trees and ferns and herbs that our people used to eat are gone. The area has been cleared. Slopes have been washed away. What will remain is a skeleton of nature.

We sacrifice the region and the environment for ten or fifteen years of development. But scars for millions of years to come will remain.

And who is benefiting right now? Not our local tribes. Not the local areas. It's not us who are able to benefit from the fruits of those mines. Nor our future generations. The money that is earned now by all that large-scale mining leaves the area and disappears into the hands of companies and institutions we cannot control. That money disappears quickly, but the scars remain, never to recover. All these places are being raped.

Our communities and environment are suffering from a development that does not benefit the local people. Oh yes, it's true, hospitals and schools are being built, and jobs are created. These are positive elements for sure. But if you take a closer look, then you see cheap labor and exploitation. The price we pay for a damaged environment is too high. We sacrifice our nature for quick money. Our leaders are selling out our land. Our natural richness is being plundered. We do not profit. And what remains are wounds that never heal. Is that development? And after that? Misery for our people. Pollution caused by chemicals has already killed pigs and even people. How many more will suffer?

It could be different. We could do the mining ourselves. Step by step. In a responsible way, with concern for the environment.

The white man sees man as the highest creature in the hierarchy. We see man as a link in the chain. And the chain is broken. Of course, man is an important creature. But he is also responsible. If he is, according to the white man, the highest creature, man should also bear the highest responsibility. Animals, trees, birds, nature—they all have rights also.

I think nature will pay back the disrespect shown to her. Look around you! It's becoming hotter, drier, more eroded. Here, in Huli country, people are hiding from the sun. They never used to do that before. The land is more barren than ever before. That's why people have to work harder. Look how skinny they are! And because of all this clearing of our forests we have floods, which we never had before. We see it here. Our fertile swamps, where we plant our *kaukau* and our sweet potatoes, they are drying out. Soon there will be no more swamps. What then? What's the cause of all this? I think it's greed. Something in humanity must be evil in itself. The ruthlessness and selfishness in a struggle for survival. The institutional organizations, big companies, and corporate bodies have become dehumanized. Profits at all costs, regardless of what that leaves behind.

I think it's still not too late. We still have a chance, if the proper leaders show their responsibility. But, of course, it's not a concern of leaders alone. The peoples of the world should rise up together—arm in arm—and act according to their responsibility for the Earth. The world should come together for the just cause. We must fight for the survival of our human society. We must fight together.

My people are naive. We, leaders and future leaders, have to make them aware of what is happening around them. And not only we, here in Huli land, but everywhere in our country, in the entire outside world. The time is ripe for a worldwide appeal. We should abandon our isolation here. We should be more connected, have more relationship to individuals and organizations and politicians and environmentalists from all around the world.

United, we should be able to pinpoint what and who is causing the most environmental damage, throughout the world. Information should be passed on about what is going on and where it is going on and who is doing what. And from that information action should be taken. We have to! We have to be aware about our survival. We have to think of our children. The language of action has to be spoken. A world environmental body should be set up, a global organization, an independent organization. Companies and governments that want to exploit natural resources should be obliged to hire independent environmental specialists. The advice of these independent specialists should be followed, not that of the so-called experts who are hired by the companies themselves.

I think if the United Nations takes responsibility for war to protect the interests of oil companies, then the United Nations has the responsibility to protect the environment of the nations of the Earth.

DAMBUTJA DATARAK
(AS TOLD TO B. WONGAR)

(Aborigine/Australia)

Iharang, the Healing Plant

Dambutja Datarak was a medicine man of an Aboriginal people near Yirkala, in northeast Arnhemland, Australia. He died of the effects of radiation poisoning in 1985. Before his death, he recounted the tragic story of his community to novelist and poet B. Wongar, a Serbian expatriate who emigrated to Australia in the 1960s and married into Datarak's people. Mr. Wongar's wife also died of radiation poisoning.

In the early 1970s, a large mining complex mushroomed out from virgin bush at Gove Peninsula, a remote part of the Arnhem Land aboriginal reserve. No road connects Gove with the rest of Australia; the nearest town is Darwin, some seven hundred kilometers west across the tribal wilderness. Nabalco Mining imported an entire mining complex by air and sea. Several thousand white workers were also brought in. Before their arrival, there were only a handful of white missionaries in the whole area.

The arriving whites moved in by ship, airplane, helicopter. They blasted the bush, horrifying every tribal soul. Our tribal people, *yuln*, lived in the Gove area for two thousand generations and were self-sufficient and culturally independent—nonaggressive.

Dambutja Datarak (Aborigine/Australia)

Scholars from all over the world frequently came to visit the Gove area to learn about our tribal poetry dating back to the beginning of time, about art, and about ritual life. Our tribal elders—Mauwulan, Nanjin, Djawa, Djunmal, and others—were often portrayed in books and papers. Yet in the original agreement leasing the tribal land at Gove to Nabalco for mining, there is no mention of our people and culture. The tribal healer, alone, had to care for both.

✦

No day passes without my hearing from my Galei (wife). She is out in the bush and howls—she does it often at night. I wake up, listen to her calls, and wonder: has she been caught in a steel trap?

I have known Galei all my life, perhaps even longer. Life stretches farther back than the day a *yuln* is born—it does not end when he dies. In Wanga (my tribal country), every soul is reborn—you could turn into a tree, a bird, or a dingo. But that was before *balanda* (white man) came. Why does Galei howl?

From Nandjaranga (sacred site) Cape and stretching westward along the coast for many camps is our tribal bush. The whites call it Arnhem Land reserve or "black man's country." I was told there are more trees and dingoes out in the bush than the whites can count. Perhaps there are more tribal souls out there than drops in the monsoon rain. I used to talk about it with Galei; that was before she left me.

I first saw Galei when she was a toddler. A large tree had fallen on the camping ground, wounding her badly. They called in Mari (my uncle), for he was *marngit* (tribal healer). The old man grabbed his dilly bag and rushed to help, taking me with him. On the way I helped him gather dry grass and branches and made a fire to spread a smoke screen. He taught me that when going to help a wounded soul, people should pass through a smoke screen so that they do not bring flies with them. We even made a fire before approaching the camp to let the smoke saturate the bush and drive away the flies and bugs. Looking yellow, Galei quivered like the discarded tail of a lizard. She had a large bleeding wound on one of her hips.

Mari crushed bulbs of the white bush lily in a bailer shell and left them to soak. Before washing the wound with that stuff, he gently removed any bits of wood and dirt hanging about; then he held the torn skin together. Over the wound he placed *mabanda* (yellow hibiscus) leaves heated on the fire. Galei kept quivering, but did not cry. Maybe she felt afraid or too weak to make a sound. The wound was wrapped with strips of *mabanda* bark. The old man asked me to bring an armful of *gadayka* (paper bark) for Galei to lie on and keep warm.

Mari sang that night, as the healer often does, calling for the ancestors from Bralgu (our spirit world) to bring help. No ancestor answered, but a sole dingo howled from the bush. "She'll live." He told me that the dingo often passed on the news from our spirit ancestors to Wanga people. I was young then, learning the secrets of healing. The old man told me that when growing into *marngit* one has to know not only the people but also *waragan*—dingoes, trees, and all other creatures: "We're the same *mala* (crowd)." I must have told Galei about it.

Lucky for Mari—at the time he was the tribal healer no *balanda* had yet settled in Wanga. Now and then a steamer would sail around Nandjaranga Cape, bellowing smoke. That floating thing looked like a drifting log set on fire. Our people thought that the *balanda* were sailing on a raft and that they had set it on fire so that they could boil their billy can and make tea. Our women and children stayed away from the coast, fearing that the steamer might drift closer and land *balanda*. I often thought of asking Mari why some of our people have to run inland from the *balanda* men, and thought he might tell me about it in time to come.

Dambutja Datarak (Aborigine/Australia)

As far back as I can remember, the people said that ever since Dreaming (the mythical time), Wanga had never had such a good healer as Mari. With him about, no *yuln* suffered very much from dislocated finger, "running belly," or high fever. The right healing plants always grew in the bush. The people often thought that he could sing life even into a tree struck by lightning.

The word about him must have gone far beyond Wanga—missionary people living some camps away down the coast often sent out a message stick with some barley sugar, which meant that his help was badly needed. Galei and I both hoped that one day he might tell me why our people ran into the bush when that steamer showed up around Nandjaranga Cape.

Mari often used to tell me how during Dreaming our Wanga was a plain of bare sand. Termite people lived then, eating trees, roots, everything. With so many of them about, the country ran out of food quickly, and they had to eat one another instead. Our spirit ancestors, who came from the sea at that time, separated the sand from the rocks and brought trees to the barren country. They made mangrove swamps, hills, rivers, and a large billabong in the middle of Wanga. Next to the billabong lay Nongaru (ceremonial ground).

Before going to Bralgu, the ancestors passed on to a *yuln* the secrets of rain. Before the arrival of the monsoon, the men gather on Nongaru to sing for the clouds. Old Mari told me the clouds are lured from the far sea to Wanga by tribal girls brought to Nongaru for their initiation. Each of them has her skin smeared with *malnar* (red ocher) and kangaroo fat. The girls rest in a grove of *iharang* bushes, waiting to enter the ceremonial ground and be broken by the tip of a boomerang to make them into women. Each of them is given *iharang* berry to taste.

Pity Galei never tasted one. She would still be with me if she had.

Mari told me that those *iharang* bushes were planted by our spirit ancestors to help women stop bearing children. If Wanga women are allowed to breed like those ant people in the mythical time, the country could grow bare again. The ancestors left behind a pack of dingoes, who rest under a boulder near the grove and howl when the dark monsoon clouds roll on to the land. "Lightning never strikes the *iharang* bush," Mari told me. That was before the *balanda* came to Wanga.

The first white man I saw in our country seemed mad about rocks.

He carried a small hammer, used to chip the flakes from boulders that he tucked into his rucksack. That man gave Mari a metal *darkgul* (hatchet) and a billy can; then he told us that both those things came from the rocks. Mari was promised that in time to come every *yuln* would receive the same gift. Old Mari had been given a metal *darkgul* by a missionary—Cross Man we called him—who lived several camps away down the coast from Nandjaranga Cape. The new hatchet looked much sharper and shinier. Although the hatchets were different, the whites looked as much like each other as turtle eggs.

We called the white man Gunda (boulder). When Galei asked me how he happened to be in our country, I could not tell. I thought, however, that he might be a *balanda* spirit brought by the monsoon clouds. I had never met a man who would go round chipping boulders. He came just before our big ceremony at Nongaru. We had already made a pile of boomerangs, smeared them with *malnar* and kangaroo fat, each ready for the sacred ritual to make a girl into a woman. My Galei was to be initiated then.

Mari asked me to lead Gunda into the far part of our country, away from Nongaru, and keep him there chipping the boulders because no stranger has ever seen our initiation ceremony. If anyone intruded on Nongaru or on our *iharang* grove, the dingoes would howl and our spears would hold him back. Poor Galei, she missed the initiation gathering—she had to accompany me to the hills to make the camp fire and gather bush tucker for me and Gunda. Pity for her—if she had been *bala* (initiated), she would not now be out in the bush, turned into a dingo and howling. I think she reminds me that Wanga—most of it—has been taken by the whites. Our poor country.

When one of us dies, his spirit splits into two parts. One part stays in the country and turns into a tree, the other goes to Bralgu Island for a while. The spirits come to the mainland now and then; turned into gnats, they hover in the air looking for a young woman who might be asking for them. A gnat appears in her dream first, and if she nods, then it enters her. However, no soul was able to be reborn in Wanga without a good family to grow up in and the land to live from.

That was how we lived when Mari was alive, and for many monsoons before that—ever since our spirit ancestors were here. That Nandjaranga Cape, which juts out into the sea like a pointed finger, was made so that the spirits of the dead could go there to wait for our Nangang (ferryman) to take them by canoe to Bralgu.

This does not happen now. The cliffs of Nandjaranga Cape have been flattened and the place turned into a jetty. The whites have built a pathway for some strong metal monster that looks like an immense serpent stretching across the country from Nongaru ground to Nandjaranga Cape. "Conveyor belt," Cross Man called the metal monster. The thing rattled day and night carrying rocks down to that jetty and pouring them into the bellies of huge ships. "The whole country could go that way," Cross Man warned me. Mari thought so too. Good that poor old Mari died some monsoons before. The day the old man went, he handed me a hatchet and billy can: "Take that to *balanda*." He told me we have our own tools we should hold on to.

Not long after the old man died, that missionary fellow Cross Man came to the bush to look for me. He told me Mari had appeared in his dreams asking that we do something to drive the mining people from Wanga: "Soon there might be no country left." Cross Man wanted me and other tribal fellows to go to *balanda* court in a faraway town and tell them what had happened to our land. He gave me a pair of shorts and a T-shirt and told me to smarten myself up: "Those people in town still think that you fellows are only part human." He told us we would make history—never before had a *yuln* gone to white man's court to fight for his land. With new clothes on we looked strange to one another, even funny—our people laughed when they gathered to see us off.

No tribal healer should put *balanda* clothes on and leave his country at a time when it is in the grip of a curse. I thought that by going to town I might see Galei. Some monsoons ago, when we were on that trip with Gunda, the white man took her away from me and fled the country. I have often seen her since then in my dreams, always ceremonially dressed. Pretty she looked, her skin smeared with *malnar* and wearing a *galamba* (armband) made of cockatoo down and possum fur. Her fast-budding breasts were held by a harness to keep them firm. She looked ready to step out on to Nongaru ground and be made into *bala* (woman). Perhaps when coming to me in my dreams she is trying to remind me that no tribal girl should enter womanhood without being properly initiated.

On the initiation ground the girls are seen by the spirits from Bralgu, who turn into gnats and hover in the air. They know to whom each of the girls is betrothed and what the country they are going to live in looks like—does it have plenty of trees, billabongs, yam, and fish? This determines how many children she is going to have—two, perhaps more if the country is vast and abundant with tucker.

The white man at the court called Judge wanted to know why we need *iharang* bush growing near Nongaru billabong. "The spirit ancestors wanted it that way." I spoke only our tribal lingo, but Cross Man was there to interpret every word I said. No other *balanda* knows our lingo.

Judge wore some kind of headdress, made from the skin of a dingo, by the look of it. He said he had heard all good things about what I did as tribal healer and tried to smile: "Your people have been poor, struggling with stone axes since the Ice Age. Surely it would be unfair to deprive them of the benefits of the hatchet and billy can." He asked me if we had a "land title" given to us by our spirit ancestors—some piece of paper I gather. Cross Man tried to explain that we neither write nor read. As for our ancestors, they lived in a mythical time when the rivers and mountains were made and the first *yuln* was born. "Is that according to our God or theirs?" the Judge wanted to know.

On our behalf, Cross Man presented the court with a large bark painting done by a group of our fellows, showing our tribal countries, plentiful with yams and animals, many of which were sacred. In the center of the picture lay Nongaru and near it *iharang* bush gathered by dingoes; that was painted solely by me in red and yellow ocher—only the tribal healer is allowed to do it. Judge looked pleased: "It's a nice picture, I will see it is hung in my library." Judge wanted to hear from me about the hatchet and billy can given to Mari by the white man, and did he make good use of it? He even asked me if any of our people eat the rocks. Perhaps that white man Gunda might have said that we gave the country away for that rusting axe and can.

I asked at the court if they could let me see my Galei. Cross Man must have misinterpreted my request, for Judge looked at me: "Sorry, but this court cannot grant you a woman." They all laughed. Perhaps they thought I was asking for a white one. Galei returned to Wanga some monsoons later. She did not come to the bush to see me but went to her *mala* (clan). It is farther on from Nandjaranga Cape, along the coast. The sea there enters through a strait hardly a good voice long and then widens into a bay that would take a man many camps to walk around. In no time one catches a barramundi there. The mangrove forest used to be packed with *njuga* (crabs). You could walk past one billabong after another, all covered with lily pads. No country was kinder to its people and more plentiful with food than Galei's. Not any longer though.

The whites have built a settlement on the shore of the bay to melt the rocks. The place rattles, always puffing something—steam or smoke. Perhaps both. The stuff smells like a clutch of turtle's eggs turned bad and burst. You could be many camps out of sight but not out of reach of the stink. The water in the bay has grown yellow or reddish. I could not be sure, for there is always a haze hanging over it. There are no barramundi to be seen; the fish have long since been washed up on the shore—dead. The mangroves do not like the place either; the trees have shed their leaves—nothing but dry skeletons. I doubt whether they make axes and billy cans out at that smelter. There are not many of us left to need them anyway.

Not even Galei keeps a billy can. She had made her home in a discarded water tank on a rubbish tip not far from the settlement. Her children looked much like her while they were still toddlers, but their skin is lighter. Some even have *bulku dilmir* (freckles) on their faces.

I saw her often on my way to the jail, whenever I went there to fetch one of our fellows. At first I thought that one of our men might be wounded and need a good cure—that's what I am for. I always carry in my dilly bag some white bush lily to stop the bleeding and treat the wounds. It always turns out that it is too late for healing—the poor fellow is stiff dead. I think they call me there only to take the bodies of our fellows into the bush. The whites do not want any of our kind to be buried on the land taken from us. Perhaps they fear that our people, when reborn, could claim the land again. Galei thought so. She told me that if any of our fellows is found hanging around the white settlement he is thrown behind a locked door. They would not lock her up though. The whites come to the rubbish tip to seek her company.

Poor Galei—there was a whole mob of children flocking around her, and there was always a new one on the way, by the look of her belly. She often came to see me in the bush, asking for *iharang* berry. I tried to tell her that Nongaru and much of the country around have been dug out. The sacred billabong has gone, so has the grove of *iharang* bushes. The whites have turned the place into a mining quarry. It looks as though some monster, never seen before, has intruded on the place, crushed the boulders, and wallowed in the dust. It is still wallowing.

At sunset a blast is often heard from Nongaru. The earth jerks upward with a cloud of dust or smoke—one can never tell.

Shaken, poor Wanga, our poor country, trembles like a badly wounded serpent. The dust cloud spits scattering rocks. They too travel across the land almost as far as the noise of the blast. I once saw a piece of wood flying into the air from Nongaru. Bent, it looked much like one of our sacred boomerangs smeared with blood. It fell halfway down the Nandjaranga Cape. Galei kept on pleading: "You're the healer, do something to help."

I found an *iharang* bush growing among the rocks at the far end of the country. It looked stunted, the leaves coated with dust. The tree had no berries on it and looked unlikely to flower ever again. I took some bark from the bush then pounded it with a rock before placing it in the bailer shell half-filled with water, and left the thing to soak. While he was around, Mari told me that if a woman drank stuff like that it would make her sick; she would recover after a while and go on to live, but without ever having children again. Poor Galei—she did not make it.

That tribal ancestor Nangang no longer comes to ferry the souls of the dead to Bralgu. The rocks down at Nandjaranga Cape have been blasted long ago. The noise from the blasts has frightened even the sea monsters. The dreadful rotting smell from the smelter hangs in the air—our spirits would stay a sky away from Wanga. Galei is out in the bush, turned into a dingo. Last night she came close to me, looking for food in my camp. She sniffed the ground around me for the crumbs left behind from my last meal; for a while I felt her hairy tail touching my face.

Before going to sleep next time, I shall leave her some yams and part of the damper (bush bread) cooked in hot ashes. She was fond of that tucker.

❋

About fifteen or so years ago, the mining town of Gove was given the *yuln* name Nhulunbuy. The town has a large hospital, school, hotel —for whites. It also has a courthouse, a police station, and a jail made of concrete in which the aborigines are often locked.

A cape near Gove bears the name of William Wilberforce, the man who pioneered the Abolition of Slavery Act 1833. The act supposedly gave rights to indigenous people over their land and culture. Lawyers in Australia are barred from referring to that legislation.

Nabalco nowadays pays some symbolic royalties to our people. We also receive government payments (pension or unemployment benefits). This money is often spent at Nhulunbuy paying police fines, or spent on alcohol, fast food, and other goods alien to our traditional life-style. The world from outside is no longer interested in our culture.

People nowadays fly to Gove to compile reports on problems to do with aboriginal health, high mortality rates, alcoholism, death in police custody, and reports on pollution and environmental decay.

If the mining corporation ever leaves Gove, the bush might reclaim some of the devastated land. That might not be so with our culture.

PABLO SANTOS

(Aeta/Philippines)

The Day the Mountain Said No

Pablo Santos is a member of the Aeta tribe and has been active in fighting for indigenous rights for various native groups in the Philippines. For this, he was detained under the previous regime of Ferdinand Marcos. He is now the secretary-general of the National Federation of the Indigenous People of the Philippines, known by its Filipino acronym, KAMP (Kalipunan Ng Mga Katutubong Mamamayan Ng Pilipinas).

When Mount Pinatubo in the Philippines erupted in June 1991, in what has turned out to be this century's most violent volcanic explosion, the Aeta people thought it was the end of their world.

The Aetas, an indigenous people who settled on the present-day island of Luzon some twenty thousand years ago, had long known their way of life was threatened—but they were sure it was going to be man's abuse of nature that would eventually deal the final blow.

They were not prepared for the day Mount Pinatubo literally blew its top off, spewing out more than eight cubic kilometers of searing rocks, lava, and dust high into the atmosphere before coming to rest within a fifty-kilometer radius of the mountain.

It was the elders who saw the eruption as the sign that Mount Pinatubo—Apo Mamalyari (Creator)—had finally said no to its desecration by man.

For thousands of years, the Aeta people had lived in the thick rain forests of the Zambales range, a jagged ridge that forms the spine along Luzon's southwestern coast. Many lived in the thick jungles on the slopes of Mount Pinatubo, and its relative remoteness sheltered the Aetas from persecution by the lowland settlers—first Malay, then Spanish. Their lives on and around what modern-day geologists had declared to be a dormant or extinct volcano, which last erupted about six hundred years ago, revolved around a fundamental principle: "Land is life."

It is a phrase that to outsiders often has sounded like a cliché or slogan. But to the indigenous people of the Philippines these are three words that describe their sacred bond with Mother Earth.

All the indigenous people of the Philippines believe they are the sons and daughters of the Earth. "The Earth is the breast that feeds us," in the words of Datu Mandagese of Agusan on the island of Mindanao over five hundred kilometers to the south of Luzon. "The land is an extension of our body. Anything that causes damage to the Earth causes the same to the Lumad [non-Muslim hill tribes in Mindanao]. When the land is abused, so are the Lumad." For the Aeta people, land cannot be bought or sold, it cannot be owned by just one person—the Earth is for everybody so that everyone can live. Why can't the Aeta sell land? Because land was created by the supreme deity for their parents, themselves, and their children. The Earth is sacred.

Long before the government officials came along, the Aeta had laws of the land through the leaders, chief, warriors, and priests that marked boundaries using mountains streams, rivers, and old trees. The land was where the ancestors were born, died, and buried. On Aeta land, the destruction of the forests began with the arrival of people who did not respect the trees and mountains. Tall, sturdy trees were replaced by smaller, fast-growing trees, and when these were harvested the land eroded. The rivers became dirty and the fish scarce. Then even the fish disappeared, because of silting in the lakes and lagoons.

For the indigenous people of the Philippines, respect for land is respect for life itself. Land and life are one and the same.

But land has always been a source of conflict. This is especially true when it has come to relations with the authorities, where the value attached to land by indigenous people is exactly the opposite of that of the government. While the indigenous people look at land as life itself, governments, past and present, look at land as a commodity. While the indigenous people look at land as a source of life for all generations, the government looks at land as a source of huge profits for a few.

Land provides not only for the physical needs of the indigenous people, it provides a line of continuity from the past to the present. It mirrors a history of struggle in defense of a homeland. Land is home. It defines the relationship of people within and outside the community.

The difference spells conflict between the government and the indigenous people, with the latter at a disadvantage. After all, the government has all the means—from laws to arms—to enforce its programs and facilitate the operations of profit-making corporations within the confines of the communal territories of the indigenous people.

Intrusion into ancestral lands and exploitation of their natural resources began as early as the country's colonization by Spain in the mid-sixteenth century.

To legitimize such plunder, land laws were enacted during the Spanish period, institutionalized during the U.S. regime toward the end of the nineteenth century, followed to the letter by succeeding pseudo-independent Philippine governments, made more repressive and exploitative under the regime of Ferdinand Marcos, and vigorously implemented under the present authorities.

These laws virtually rendered the indigenous people squatters on their own lands. And it was these laws that gave the Philippine government the "right" to prospect for geothermal energy on Mount Pinatubo, drilling deep into the mountain to tap the heat in its bowels.

Not only that, the sides of the mountain were full of illegal loggers and poverty-stricken lowland peasants nibbling away at Pinatubo's last remaining forests. At the same time, war planes from the nearby U.S. Clark Air Base used a valley below the mountain for target practice, and the Aetas had long grown accustomed to the thunder of low-flying jets and earthshaking explosions.

So our elders were not surprised when the earth heaved and the mountain threw its bowels out into the surrounding atmosphere, some of the dust circling the globe and reddening sunsets on the other side of the planet.

No one yet has a precise count, but as many as one hundred Aeta perished as the first pyroclastic flows snuffed out the forests and enveloped their flimsy huts. Those who ran to nearby caves or fled down the mountain were saved. Of the estimated thirty thousand Aetas living on Pinatubo, about seventeen thousand are now in an evacuation center in Baquilan on the coast. Here the Philippine government is trying to assimilate the Aetas into life in the lowlands.

For a community that was already at the threshold of cultural extinction, the eruption of Pinatubo has hastened the demise of the tribal ways in which the natural environment meant everything.

The Aetas' strong oral tradition passed knowledge and skills about jungle survival from generation to generation. Every valley, river, rock outcrop, or tree on Pinatubo had a significance in Aeta lore.

Today, deposits as thick as two hundred meters cover some valleys. Military helicopter pilots who have flown over the crater describe scenes like those seen on other planets. Aeta elders say Apo Mamalyari (the Creator) was angry at man's abuse of nature, like the geothermal drilling, the bombing by the jets, and the denudation of forests on the sacred mountain. Their alien and squalid life in the camps is now seen as the punishment of Pinatubo.

The Aetas themselves were nomadic and later practiced shifting agriculture—burning a small area of forest, growing root crops in the ashes, and moving on. But their traditional slash-and-burn practice has always been carefully done to give time for nature to renegerate itself. All natural things, living and nonliving, are believed to be inhabited by spirits that cannot be offended.

Modern Western anthroplogists have studied the Aetas, and the U.S. military even used their knowledge of jungle survival to train U.S. soldiers during the Vietnam War. The Aetas have a vast storehouse of knowledge of the species of plant and animal life on the mountain and are able to identify four hundred and fifty types of plants and even twenty species of ants.

But, after generations of freedom, the Aetas now have a hard time coming to grips with camp life. They even look uncomfortable in the trousers and T-shirts supplied by relief agencies. Almost six hundred Aetas, mostly children, died in the camps in the five months following the eruption. They lack immunity to lowland diseases like measles, pneumonia, and malaria, and many have succumbed to diarrheal dehydration. Without access to their forest herbs, the Aetas have not been able to administer their traditional medications. Aeta shamans are also hesitant to perform their healing rituals because camp officials make fun of them.

Looked at in historical perspective, the eruption of Mount Pinatubo seems like the final crushing blow against the Aetas. These people, described by anthropologists as a small, black, kinky-haired people who are ethnic cousins of the Australian aborigines, had already suffered enough.

Lowland chauvinism, discrimination, and greed for land had already forced the Aetas to retreat farther and higher up the mountains. Aeta ancestral grounds, even in the early nineteenth century, were eyed for housing, agricultural, and commercial settlements for the lowlanders—the Unat, or "people with straight hair."

Since then, the appropriate laws in place, and bombs and bullets ready, transnational and multinational corporations have ravaged the resources within the ancestral lands of the indigenous people. A long list of corporations—in the logging, mining, agribusiness and plantation sectors—cling like leeches to Aeta ancestral lands, considered by the government the final frontier for extracting resources to make a profit.

Seeing one's land raped by foreigners is enraging. For it to be done with the full blessing of the government is unbearable. To facilitate and attract corporate profit-making, the government has built dams, geothermal plants, roads, and bridges as support and complementary mechanisms. All of this is viewed by the indigenous people as an assault on life itself, a direct cause of environmental destruction. It is a case of greed subverting life, they say.

Take the case of another of the Philippines' mountains, Mount Apo, or Apo Sandawa to the tribes living in the area. Mount Apo, the Philippines' highest mountain peak, is not just a tourist spot or a laboratory for the scientist interested in biodiversity. To the Lumads of the area it is much more—it is a sacred place, similar to the Christian's cathedral. But the government did not consider it sacrilegious when it allowed blasting on parts of the sacred mountain and felled hundreds of trees to put up a geothermal plant to supply 23 percent of Mindanao's electricity requirements. All in the name of development.

Under the administration of Ferdinand Marcos, mining and timber companies, plantation owners, settlers, and traders were given first priority. Back in Luzon, reservations established by the government in the province of Pampanga were sorry substitutes for resource-rich ancestral lands. The Aetas had been resisting "development aggression" on Mount Pinatubo long before it erupted.

In the 1980s, the Philippine national oil company dug three wells to prospect for geothermal energy sources, evicting Aetas from the region in the process. When the wells proved unproductive, the oil company abandoned them but did not bother to prevent or monitor the possible environmental consequences of the drilling. Aeta elders say the vents of the three wells have been emitting sulphuric steam. They think there is a connection between this and the cataclysmic eruption of June 1991.

The forests immediately surrounding the wells had already been killed by the vapors, the soil had become powdery white and acidic, and the rivers that provided the Aetas with water had become muddy and foul-smelling. One nine-year-old girl even died after drinking the water.

Then there is the problem of the U.S. military bases. Although it has been decided not to renew their leases, much damage has already been done. The Aetas have birthright claims over vast areas occupied by the big U.S. military bases in the Philippines—the air force base at Clark and the Subic Bay naval base. In 1910, the establishment of the Clark air base led to massive land-grabbing schemes and forced the Aetas to move higher up the slopes of Mount Pinatubo.

In 1954, during the laying of the foundations for the Subic naval station, scores of Aeta communities succumbed to promises of better livelihood chances in resettlement areas. Since 1900 they have been forced to relocate four or five times.

Aetas living on the fringes of the camps have been shot and killed indiscriminately by U.S. guards while scavenging among the garbage. Records of how Aeta children were shot after being mistaken for wild boar, or how elderly tribeswomen were bitten by fierce guard dogs, only serve to highlight the extensive suffering and humiliation inflicted on the Aetas by the Americans—long after the Philippines became officially independent of U.S. colonial rule.

The resistance of the indigenous people to these so-called developments is often viewed as an expression of nothing more than sentiment for days and times gone by. The indigenous people reply that they are neither sentimentalists nor antidevelopment. If there is a segment of the population that wants development, it is theirs. What they do not want are the projects rammed down their throats by the government. "Projects implemented by the government and those they allow to operate in ancestral areas are not for development," says Kalipunan Ng Mga Katutubong Mamamayan Ng Pilipinas (KAMP), the National Federation of the Indigenous People of the Philippines. "How could these projects lead to development if they cause the displacement of the people who are supposed to be their beneficiaries?"

In January 1990, KAMP, together with minority rights advocacy groups, launched the Campaign against Development Aggression to call the attention of the government and public to the various development projects mushrooming in ancestral areas. "The so-called development projects being implemented by the government only deplete the remaining resources of the country, in addition to causing environmental degradation that adds to the debt burden of the country," KAMP argues.

Even the government's Integrated Social Forestry Program (ISFP), supposedly one of the pillars of the government's campaign for refor-estation, has been criticized by the indigenous people because it is being implemented with blatant disregard for ancestral land rights. In essence, the logic of the program is to render indigenous people squat-ters and to reduce their role to mere caretakers instead of owners of the land. The so-called development projects cause massive problems among indigenous people, who end up as sacrificial lambs on the gov-ernmental altar of development.

A slain indigenous leader, Macliing-Dulag, once said: "If life is threatened, what should a man do? Resist. This he must do, otherwise he is dishonored, and that is a worse death. If we do not fight . . . we die anyway. If we fight we die honorably. I exhort you all then—fight."

The indigenous people of the Philippines believe land must be defended against the continued rape by foreign and local big business engaged in logging, mining, chemical-dependent agribusiness planta-tions, and destructive government projects that continue to threaten the life of all Philippine residents.

"We have always been careful with the Earth," says Datu Makalipay of Agusan in Mindanao. "We will struggle to make sure no one takes what remains of our forests. I will defend our land to prevent further abuse and exploitation of its remaining wealth."

To defend land is to defend life. This is the heart of the indigenous people's struggle. Already there have been some small victories. In Mindanao, for example, there are some six thousand hectares of an-cestral lands in South Cotabato that have been reoccupied by B'laan, Bagobo, and Manobo people.

"These lands were taken from us through brute force and decep-tion," says Lumad Mindanaw, the regional alliance of indigenous people in Mindanao.

Land reoccupation signals a new level in the struggle of the indigenous people of the Philippines, who are tired of the government's empty promises and the endless cycle of petition letters to government representatives. In the words of Lumad Mindanaw, it is an "assertion of our ancestral rights."

The problem is that these efforts are not welcome. The people are harassed and silenced. In November 1990, some one hundred and ninety houses were strafed and burned in Laconon, South Cotabato, and fourteen T'boli and B'laan were tortured.

"We know now that our struggle to survive exacts a high price. But we are willing to sacrifice anything to defend the source of our life—our land. It will ensure the existence and the future of the next generations," says Lumad Mindanaw.

As Macliing-Dulag said, "To claim a place is the birthright of every man. The lowly animals claim their place. How much more man?" That birthright became all the more difficult to claim the day after the mountain heaved its boiling intestines into the Philippine skies.

Tension has been building between the Aetas and the lowland refugees of Mount Pinatubo, with lowlanders maintaining that the Aetas have been given preference in relief efforts. Some lowlanders have threatened to harass and bomb Aeta evacuation centers. The hostility has led some Aetas to retreat back into what remains of the forests on the foothills of the volcano, where they are trying to pick up the pieces of their lives among the skeletons of the scarred trees on the slopes of ash-covered hills. History has documented that rather than come into conflict with the people of the lowlands, the Aetas would rather go farther back into the forests and live once again as a docile and peace-loving people.

The Aetas, like the other indigenous groups of the Philippines, and indeed of much of Southeast Asia, consider the land to be their life, particularly ancestral lands where natural objects and landmarks are part of their tradition and lore. Having lost their last bastion, the Aetas face an uncertain future in the refugee camps that ring the mountain. And many Aetas have shown that instead of leading a diminished life in the evacuation centers, they would rather risk the desolate landscape and return to their ancient lands to start again to live as their ancestors did.

SARATH KOTAGAMA

(Buddhist/Sri Lanka)

Practice What You Preach:
A Lesson for Sustainable Living

Dr. Sarath Wimalabandara Kotagama, a Sri Lankan zoologist, was director of the Department of Wildlife Conservation in the Sri Lankan Ministry of Lands, Irrigation, and Mahaweli Development. He has acted as a resource person in environmental education for the UN Environment Program (UNEP) and is a member of the Commission on National Parks and Protected Areas of the International Union for the Conservation of Nature (IUCN). He is now associated with the Open University of Sri Lanka.

In the centuries-long race to become "developed," the pursuit of "modernization," "civilization," and all the other attributes of "development" became cause and motive for sweeping aside universal truths that govern the relationship between the human species and nature. Life itself became expendable in the name of "development." Nature could be destroyed and people could be shifted around, like pawns on a chess board.

But now, as we come to the end of the twentieth and enter the twenty-first century, the human species is showing some signs of rediscovering its lost identity, to gauge from a joint initiative launched in October 1991 by the International Union for the Conservation of

Nature (IUCN), the UN Environment Program (UNEP), and the Worldwide Fund for Nature (WWF). Representatives from the three organizations in sixty countries have drawn up an agenda for change from the disastrous actions of the past, having seen that the experiment man has carried out has opened his eyes to the ills of his own action. The agenda, known as Caring for the Earth—A Strategy for Sustainable Living, is based on a series of principles and concrete actions aimed at a new approach to living that meets two fundamental requirements: "commitment to a new ethic, the ethic for sustainable living" and "integration of conservation and development."

To date, the strategy for development and civilization that the world has practiced, preached, and propagated has run completely counter to the principle of respect and care for the community of life. Sri Lanka embraced Buddhism in the third century B.C., and since then our culture, religion, and society have tried to follow this principle. Reverence and respect for life became an integral component of our lives. No leader could remain in his position and rule if he did not agree to follow Buddhist precepts.

The first and foremost precept is, "Do not destroy life." How strange that the consciousness now being expressed about the need for sustainable living and the integration of conservation and development had already been formulated all those centuries ago, when mankind realized that the most important element for good living is respect for other life-forms.

Protection of the forests, of life, were part and parcel of the day-to-day living of our peoples. The rulers of the nation were respected and allowed to rule only if they practiced this principle.

Before the advent of Buddhism, hunting of animals for fun was an accepted pastime of royalty, as aptly demonstrated by King Devanampiyatissa, who was "caught in the act" by Arahat Mahinda. But once the learned king embraced Buddhism, everything changed. In fact, legend has it that his hunting area, Mihintale, was set aside as a sanctuary for living beings. It continues as a sanctuary to this day, making it probably the oldest recorded area in the world set aside as a refuge to protect animals.

From that moment on, the history of Sri Lanka has no records of royalty or regional leaders indulging in "killing for fun." In fact, this principle of not destroying life is so deeply ingrained in the traditional social system that any person who does otherwise is considered a social outcast. That person is not permitted to enter Buddhist temples, to join congregations of senior citizens, or to attend social functions.

Reverence for life was so strong that norms and rules were laid down that help explain some of the practices presently followed by the Buddhist clergy, farmers, and others. For example, the *Vinaya Pitaka* (a book containing rules for monks) indicates clearly that the destruction of plants amounts to misconduct. In *vanan cideta marukkan*, Buddhism calls on its followers to "destroy the forest of derailments, not the forest of trees."

Looking back at the life history of Lord Buddha, it is very strange that all the important events in his life—birth, attainment of Buddhahood (enlightenment), his first and many other sermons, and his *parinibbana* (passing away)—happened under a tree. Buddha's first act after attaining enlightenment was to show his gratitude to the tree that had provided shelter throughout his meditation. It is said he did this by "looking at the tree for a week without blinking," a feat that is unthinkable, even impossible. Nevertheless, it is the concept that reveals the heart of Buddhism.

The Buddha preached the importance of the need to protect nature and plants. In the "Samyutta Nikaya" of the *Sutra Pitakaya*, he says that growing plants is a highly meritorious act, probably because it meets many basic needs of man. He also said that "the tree is a peculiar organism, giving shelter even to the axeman who will cut it."

Throughout history, kings have followed this enlightened vision of plant life, as exemplified by the stone inscriptions of India's Emperor Dharmasoka, who always acted in conformity with Buddhist principles. In pillar inscription number five, he passed a decree prohibiting the burning of forests. In the Girnor Rock inscription, animals in the kingdom were protected.

Under Buddhism, plants of benefit to humans were grown on the roadside. Groves were created, and trees were grown specially to provide shade for these plants. All this indicates clearly that the conservation of plants and respect for life was very much part of the Buddhist life-style. But the question is whether this attitude prevailed after the period of Lord Buddha. It was definitely present during the period of Emperor Dharmasoka in India, and thereafter in Sri Lanka after Buddhism had been embraced.

In Sri Lanka, there are records of the first mass tree-planting during the reign of Matusiva (310–250 B.C.). Furthermore, ever since it was first brought to Sri Lanka more than twenty-two hundred years ago, the sacred bo tree (*Ficus religosa*) has been carefully nurtured under royal endowment. It is likely that the bo tree has the longest recorded history of any tree in the world today, as well as being the most revered. Even to this day, it is looked after by the state.

The first recorded law to protect wildlife throughout the entire island was promulgated by Amanda Gamini Abhaya (A.D. 22–31), while veterinary surgery was practiced even by kings, and all citizens were called on to care for and give protection to animals.

Many tales indicate the degree of protection afforded to animals. There is the story of King Elara's son being punished for running over a calf. The cow then apparently went to the palace and rang the bell seeking justice, which was meted out by the king even though the accused was his own son. This reverence and respect for all living beings filters down into almost every aspect of the Sri Lankan life-style.

In agricultural practices, there was always a place for *satha-sivpawa* (mammals and other animals). Before setting fire to areas that had been cleared of trees and brush, farmers move around the bush, beating it and calling on the *satha-sivpawa* to leave the area because it would be set on fire. These traditional practices prevailed in Sri Lanka up to almost the middle of the twentieth century.

At the same time, biological control of pests was the order of the day. An extreme practice that is still recommended today is that of leaving a part of a field for the pests to feed on—birds in the paddy (rice) fields. All fields had a demarcated area referred to as the *kurulu palu* (bird loss) sector. Elsewhere, plant deterrents such as the *margosa* (which yields the bitter *nim*-oil) were used.

Against this background, it was very difficult, if not impossible, to find people willing to cultivate or look after animals for food. This can be seen even today among fisherfolk and animal herders, most of whom are non-Buddhists. Of course, this does not mean there are no Buddhists in this sort of trade, but they are very, very few.

With the colonization of Sri Lanka by Western, especially British, culture, the outlook on fauna and flora and respect for life changed completely. Trades and practices that had previously been considered unethical came to be portrayed as sport. Game hunting became a gentleman's pastime. This led to a radical change in society, where such activities became transformed into symbols of development and civilization.

Trees and forests in Sri Lanka were earmarked primarily for timber value, not for environmental needs. It is common practice today, when implementing development plans, to first send in the heavy machinery to raze and flatten everything, then build the infrastructures and set aside the fields, and then go back to replanting or reforesting vital areas.

How stupid. Why can plans not first identify the areas that need to remain as forests and then go about the necessary development activities? This was how things happened during Sri Lanka's most prosperous period. *Culavamsa* (Colombo: The Ceylone Government Information Department, 1953), a translation of part of the Mahavamsa, documents the example of King Parakramabahu in the Pancayojana district, where there were great swamps. "He took the water from there and conveyed it to rivers, laid out fields, and collected a large quantity of grain . . . he determined everywhere what was to remain as wilderness and, assembling all the village chiefs, he entrusted the inhabitants with cultivation of the remaining land." (page 281). This is undoubtedly a good lesson for most of today's planners and developers.

Today we are attempting to promote the concept of "sustainable development," meaning development that meets the needs of the present generation without compromising the aspirations and needs of the future. But looking at current development and resource use, it is sad to note that these have never been promoted in the context of the needs of future development. It was always a question of meeting the needs of the present generation with little if any reference to the future generations.

It was this that left us with millions of hectares of degraded land, the loss of biodiversity, and a cry for "sustainability," even if this latter can hardly be said to be anything new. In Sri Lanka, the question of sustainable development was part and parcel of the traditional lifestyle and was recognized by enlightened rulers who saw that environmental stability is a prerequisite for development.

Again, it is King Parakramabahu, quoted in Geiger's translation of *Culavamsa,* who said that "in the realm that is subject to me, there are not only many strips of land where crops are nourished mainly by rainwater, but a few fields which are dependent on rivers with permanent flow or on great reservoirs. Also, by many mountains, by thick jungles and widespread swamps, my kingdom is lined and divided. Truly in such a country not even a little drop of water that comes from the rain must flow into the ocean without being made useful by man." (ibid, page 277.)

Could there be any better lesson than this for rational, wise use of a resource? This is the foundation of sustainability. Ideas like these were not just abstractions, but practical ideas that have always been applied in Sri Lanka. Take the emphasis placed on ground cover: "In my kingdom, wherever it may be, there shall not be even a small courtyard without its roofing of leafage; and here and there charming parks laid out, filled full with numerous species of creepers and trees which bear fruits and which bear blossoms, and which offer many delights and which are beautified by all kinds of garden beds." (ibid, page 281–2.)

This clearly shows the understanding of tree cover and the need for vegetation. The average Sri Lankan, influenced by similar practical ideas, ensured maximum utilization of land. Today we advocate "community forestry" and "social forestry," for example, as means to overcome the problem of deforestation. Much of our forest cover is destroyed to support the "developed" world. But the resources cannot meet the demand, and so they are overexploited and destroyed.

In traditional villages, the forests were community property of various types. There were the *rajasathu,* or crown property forests, with limited use by private individuals. There were the *thahanchi kale,* or protected forests, where not even a piece of downed wood was permitted to be collected. Then there were the forests that were protected for defensive purposes, and so on.

Today we are trying to encourage communities to manage their own resources. Yet this was the practice in our traditional culture, all of which was changed with the foreign occupation of the country. All resources were to be exploited for profit in the West. The forests in the hill country were cleared, first for coffee and subsequently for tea. Cash crops were introduced, but now, many years later, we are saying these areas should be protected and forested.

After the British occupation everything changed very rapidly. By the 1920s, the Waste Land Ordinance had been enacted, and all land came under the state, representing a break with the traditional communal property system. This was undoubtedly a major contributory factor in present attitudes toward land use, though we hope to be able to revert to having the community manage its own common property.

For over two thousand years traditional Sri Lankan society had been strongly influenced by Buddhism and had lived in harmony with nature, practicing the very principles that the world now wants future generations to adopt.

Today people are beginning to realize that the rapid deterioration of the environment and the adaptation of society to the "development" strategy of the last century changed social attitudes, breaking established traditions. Today we are calling on the nations and the peoples of the world to change personal attitudes and practices. "To adopt the ethic for living sustainably, people must reexamine their values and alter their behavior. Society must promote values that support this ethic and discourage those that are incompatible with the sustainable way of life" (from *Caring for the Earth: A Struggle for Sustainable Living*. Gland, Switzerland: IUCN/UNEP/WWF, 1991).

To whom is this call addressed? The ethic for sustainable living has always been part of our cultures, and the people lived in line with such a way of life. It was the Western materialistic-consumerist strategy, considered the essence of "development," that shattered the foundation of sustainable living that is basic to our cultures. Such an ethic was considered counterproductive in modern development strategy.

For almost two centuries, Western society saw only the idea of exploiting every possible resource, in any part of its conquered world, to develop a social structure that no longer matches current global goals. These "social gains" were portrayed as the symbols of development, but are now being questioned.

This overexploiting, materialistic, unsustainable society, which was the epitome of development, now stands revealed for an unequal use of resources to attain these ends. It is, for example, a well-known fact that the present-day achievements of the "developed world" (accounting for 20 percent of the entire world) are based on using almost 80 percent of existing world resources. Almost every country in the world is exploiting material to sustain the "developed life-style."

Unfortunately, we in the "developing world" have had to discard our traditions and join the mainstream. The almost "independent economy" that was part of the "sustainable resource-use strategy" was replaced by the "dependent economy" and the life-style of "unsustainable resource use."

The call, therefore, to change attitudes and practices can only be implemented by example. Any positive change for the future of developing countries along the lines of sustainable living will be extremely difficult if those who contributed most to the cause of destruction do not make the first changes.

Yathavadi thathacari, thathacari yathavadi—practice what you preach; preach what you practice. This is the only way, and it has to be the West that changes first.

PADAM SINGH GHALEY
(AS TOLD TO KANAK DIXIT)

(Gurung/Nepal)

It's a Long Way from Barpak to Kathmandu

Padam Singh Ghaley is a mountaineer and guide, who currently lives in the Nepali capital, Kathmandu. He often travels into the Himalayan hinterland in search of new territory and to discover the wide variety of people who inhabit the deep valleys. He is a director of the Mandala trekking agency.

I was born in the Barpak Valley, deep in Nepal's Himalayan country, a member of the Gurung ethnic group that inhabits the central rib of Nepal.

My ancestors tilled these slopes, hunted on the steep mountain flanks, and gathered forest products, maintaining themselves on the land. While there was some trade in basic goods, they did not rely on assistance from the world that lay outside Barpak's hilly boundaries.

That way of life survived for centuries, until the government suddenly opened up Nepal in the 1950s. The transformation that has taken place on the face of the land and in the minds of the people since then is unprecedented. And my life is, in a sense, a mirror of the dislocation that has jostled Gurung society down to its very moorings.

As a boy, I herded goats and gathered honey in the deep forests of

Barpak. My family ate according to what the land produced, and sometimes went hungry. Our concerns were those of the Gurungs of Barpak Valley—planting and harvest, monsoon and winter, death rituals and birth celebrations. The outside world rarely intruded.

Barpak is a high valley of twelve or thirteen villages, inhabited entirely by Gurungs, a Tibeto-Burman race that probably migrated eastward from China or south from Tibet about five hundred years ago. They speak the Gurung *bhasa* (tongue), but in a dialect that Gurungs from adjacent valleys find hard to follow.

The valley is nestled so tightly against the Himalayan peaks of the Gorkha Himal range that you cannot see the mountain tops, though a short walk will bring you to the glaciers. Barpak lies two-and-a-half days' hard hike from Gorkha Bazaar, the hill principality from which the forces of Prithvi Narayan, tenth ancestor of Nepal's present King Birendra, fanned out to forcibly unify Nepal in the mid-sixteenth century.

The long-established Gurung tradition of demarcating private and common land was by planting vegetation or constructing mud walls to mark the boundaries of the terraces that crisscross the hill slopes, some of them at forty-five degrees. Even today, a farmer's land can often stretch from the bottom of the mountain to the top—a vertical distance of more than three hundred meters—and the village is usually situated above the fields on south-facing slopes. Above the houses are the pastures, and on the mountain's ridges the forests.

It is the elders of the Gurung villages who make policy, deciding which pastures are eligible for grazing, which part of the forest may be felled for old trees, which forest can be picked clean of undergrowth vegetation for fodder and which for dry and dead twigs.

A similar system also exists among the Sherpas of the Mount Everest region and the Rais and Limbus of eastern Nepal. In the remote valleys of the Nepal Himalaya, the system still works well. But where isolation has given way to an influx of outsiders and lowlanders along the age-old trekking trails, the fragile conservation system has been disturbed and erosion has set in.

At the same time, the nationalization of all forests in the 1950s dealt a major blow to the conservation practices of the Sherpas and the Gurungs. Suddenly forests were a free-for-all because they belonged to the state. The government in Kathmandu has now realized its mistake and is trying to reinstate village ownership. Wherever this has worked, it has been because the district forest officer has understood the traditional protection practices and has worked to get the village elders involved in planning and decision making about forest use.

Like other Himalayan tribes, the Gurungs still practice a sound system of alternate grazing in upland pastures. During the monsoon season, great herds of cattle, sheep, and goats head up the Seti River valley to pastures on the slopes of Mount Annapurna. Here, each village is alloted sections of the lush grazing land. Tribespeople set up temporary huts, milk their cows, produce cheese, butter, and a special long-lasting dairy product called *khurpa*.

Across the mountains in eastern Nepal, the Sherpas of the Arun Valley do the same, taking their yaks in great caravans to grazing commons in the isolated Barun Valley. And in the Khaptad region of western Nepal, there are at least twenty thousand head of cattle grazing during the rainy season on the green plateau of this four-thousand-meter-high massif.

It is interesting that despite the great number of cattle involved, they cause relatively little environmental damage. On Khaptad, pastures are never overgrazed, and the big cattle owners do not have much more say about where their livestock graze than the smaller ones. The system is egalitarian. Collective decisions are taken about where to go, how long to stay, and where to return next year. And nature's capacity of regeneration in these high mountain valleys is remarkable. By the next rainy season the pastures are lush again.

But I am no longer part of that way of life. Today, I live in the capital and travel the world as a mountaineer and guide.

In Barpak, those who always knew enough to rely on their own abilities are now beginning to sit back and look toward development projects and government rations. Like the other ethnic groups of the hills of Nepal, Gurung eyes are turned to the glittering lights of Kathmandu city.

There is one contact that the Gurungs have maintained with the outside world since the early 1800s—their recruitment as fighting soldiers, as Gurkhas, in the Indian and British armies. But not the villages of Barpak. Even though one of the most famous recipients of the Victoria Cross, Gajey Ghaley, comes from the Barpak village of Danda Gaon, the valley population as a whole had always preferred to remain in isolation. This probably helps explain their destitution today. The pressure of overpopulation had begun to make itself felt in Barpak toward the turn of the century. Without the cash infusion of Gurkha recruitment, the quality of life plummeted. As the number of people relying on the same land and the same forests increased beyond earlier levels, the locals had to adjust somehow. Now, when food runs out or hailstones destroy the *makai* (maize) and *kodo* (barley) crops, the villagers descend to the lower valleys, looking for cash income as manual laborers in development projects or road building or as porters for tourists.

My father and many other families adjusted by doing something that their ancestors had had no reason to do. They sold their meager property at a pittance and headed south, toward the plains of Chitwan. This migration was the first of its sort in the history of the Gurungs.

When word came to Barpak that the government had opened up the jungles of Chitwan, my father and others saw no reason to wait. Chitwan is a low and undulating valley where the Indo-Gangetic plains are met by the sharp ramparts of the Mahabharat Lekh. In the 1950s, Chitwan, like most of the strips of plains adjacent to the mountains (known as the *tarai*), was made up of unbroken wild habitat that hosted a profusion of flora and fauna. Under the canopy of sal and *sisham* trees and in the grasslands, Chitwan was home to the great one-horned rhinoceros, the royal Bengal tiger, leopards, the blue bull, wild boar, langur monkeys, and an incredible variety of snakes, insects, and butterflies.

But for all its wild splendor, this stretch of jungle was hardly popular with the hill men of Barpak. Since as long as they could remember, they had feared the *char kosay jhadi*, mile upon mile of unbroken close-canopied forests. It was here that the mysterious vapors of the dreaded *aulo* caught up with hill men and women foolish enough to venture down to the plains. They sweated, they shivered, and they died. The *aulo* killed highlanders, but left the local indigenous population of Tharus untouched.

Traditionally, the poorer Gurungs and Magars of the hills used to go down to the *tarai* to collect *rasan pani* (rations such as calico, salt, kerosene) for themselves as well as for the Newar Sahus (merchants originally from Kathmandu who manned the trading posts of central Nepal, such as Bandipur and Gorkha). It took eight days of nonstop walking from Barpak, following the Gandaki River, to arrive at Narayan Ghat, which served as a depot and staging point. For this was where the river emerged from the mountain gorge into the elevated plains of Chitwan, and traders and porters were able to cross the turbulent river on small, unstable dugout canoes.

On the other side, one entered the great Chitwan jungle, and twelve days of walking through its dense undergrowth led to the railhead of Narkatiya Ganj in India. It was a risky crossing. Some were mauled or killed by tigers, bitten by scorpions or snakes, or set upon by bandits as they neared India. But many more were claimed by the *aulo*. As my father, a veteran of many crossings, used to say: *"Jyan ko maya marera matra gainthyo"* (We never knew whether we'd come back alive).

Such was the desperation of my father and other poor families of Barpak, that even the fear of *aulo* did not prevent them from migrating down to the plains. *Aulo,* of course, was malaria, and it was only providence that at this very time a massive malaria eradication campaign organized by the government and the World Health Organization (WHO), as one of the first development programs in a newly opened Nepal, managed to control *aulo* and save thousands of lives. But ridding the *tarai* of *aulo* spelled the doom of the great forests, which were until then among the most untouched and richest in all of Asia.

My mother had died young, leaving me and a brother two or three years older. So when it came time to move, my father took us down with him as the very first group of settlers to leave Barpak. And we were among the first to fell the forests of Chitwan, which today is only a tiny sliver of what it was then. This was a process repeated all across Nepal's *tarai.* The once abundant forests are all gone. The poverty of the Nepali hills was changing the face of the Nepali plains.

I must have been about twelve or thirteen when my father married a second time in Chitwan. My stepmother's first child was born the following year, leaving my brother and me with the feeling of being uncared for, so I decided to go back to Barpak. Alone, hungry, and penniless, I crossed the Narayan Ghat ferry and walked for days to my grandparents in Barpak. They were as poor as my parents, and I was soon helping them manage the farm. My job was to shepherd a handful of goats, cut fodder in the forest, and help in plantings and during the harvest. When the harvest was in, my grandparents used to divide up the *alu* (potatoes), *makai* (maize), and *kodo* (barley) into different sacks, to be consumed during different months. If one lot was finished before its time, rather than dip into the next lot, we used to go into the forest and gather tubers, nettles, and berries.

But Barpak could not keep me. Having seen the outside world, even at that age, I was impatient to move on. I could also sense something happening in the Nepali hills that made the urge stronger—the rumblings of development could be heard even in the remote hillsides. The plane flights to Gorkha's small airstrip increased, carrying everything from cement bags to administrators, Western engineers, and tourists. Kathmandu had become the new center of our universe.

As the so-called development decades began in the mid-1960s, Kathmandu became increasingly important to our lives. It was Kathmandu that decided who would get a suspension bridge, a road, an agricultural project, or an airstrip. Bubble-top helicopters of the U.S. Agency for International Development (AID) mission in Kathmandu flew all over the hills, bringing wheat seeds and trying to convince us to eat *roti* (unleavened wheat bread) instead of our traditional *dhindo* (maize paste).

A Chinese-aided project broke a road all the way through the deep valleys from Kathmandu to Pokhara, passing three days south of Barpak. The word went out that there was work to be had. I had already been out of Barpak and was straining to leave again, so I needed no great persuasion to leave and go down to work as a laborer on the Kathmandu-Pokhara highway which passed a day's walk south of Gorkha. In other countries, they built roads for trade, industry, and access. In Nepal, we brought in roads only to be modern. A road meant that we were developing.

The Chinese engineers took the path of least resistance and cut the road alongside the Trisuli River. This meant that the sides were steep and that landslides would be a constant problem. But nobody asked any questions. We were too busy doing surveys, dynamiting the mountains, and dumping the rocks and the dirt over the side into the river. Since Western countries had roads and were developed, we too would build roads and we would develop.

After two years of breaking stones, it was time to move on. I drifted back down to Narayan Ghat, which was by then taking on the character of a little township. What had been a collection of shanties by the riverside had developed into a bustling jumble of permanent buildings on two sides of a wide, potholed avenue. There was even a plane service from nearby Bharatpur. Douglas DC-3 Dakotas ferried passengers to and from Kathmandu and Gorkha.

I got work as a cook and menial, or orderly, then graduated to running tractors for farmers who had cut out large tracts of forest land but did not have the manpower to till them. I worked as a tractor hand for a few years before I finally got the chance to visit Kathmandu.

An old farmer I worked for in Bharatpur, who made butter instead of *ghiu* (clarified butter), which was what all other dairy farmers produced, kept urging me to visit Kathmandu with two tins of butter to see if they would take his produce. I bought a forty-rupee air ticket to Kathmandu and carried with me two kerosene tins full of the man's butter. As the piston-engined Dakota roared off Bharatpur's grass airfield, I prayed to all my ancestors' spirits and to all the Hindu gods that I had come to know down among the Chetris, Bahuns, and Newars with whom I had lived. When we landed in Kathmandu, a virtual Hong Kong to my Barpak eyes, I headed for Lainchaur, the neighborhood where the national dairy was situated, and managed to sell the man's butter for 150 rupees a tin. After that, I became a regular commuter on the Kathmandu-Bharatpur flight, a butter trader.

Kathmandu's pull did not abate, and I started hanging out with some Chitwan friends who were going to the Tri Chandra College. There I met a couple of friends interested in climbing. The three of us, using a rock-climbing manual stolen from a local bookshop, became the first persons to explore the rocks around Kathmandu Valley, as a sport. We discovered rocks over by Pashupati Nath Temple, where the Bagmati River emerged from a gorge, and another, better, rock face over by the holy forest sanctuary of Nagarjun.

Rock climbing took me into trekking and mountaineering, which finally became my way of getting back to my mountain roots after more than fifteen years of breaking rocks, driving tractors, and trading in butter. Starting out as a boy of the Nepali outback, I had detoured through a spectrum of job opportunities in a newly developing nation and had come full circle to work in the new field of "adventure tourism."

Formerly known to foreigners as the "forbidden kingdom," Nepal started becoming a tourists' haven in the mid-1960s. Within a decade, however, the hospitable mountain people of Nepal and the enchanting terrain led to the emergence of trekking, a type of tourism unique to Nepal. With the help of porters and guides, tourists are able to hike along the main trails of Nepal, the two most popular being one that winds up the Khumbu Valley into Sherpa country to the southern base camp of Mount Everest and another that snakes up the deep gorge of the Kali Gandaki River and around the Annapurna mountain range.

I signed on as a porter in 1975, carrying tourists' belongings, bedding, kitchen utensils, and tents. The following year, I trained as a trekking guide, a *sirdar*. I traveled to far corners of the country, always trying out trails other than the well-trodden ones.

I didn't realize it then, but the arrival of mass tourism in the form of trekking was leaving an indelible mark on the Annapurna trail, as well as on the Barun Valley, and to a lesser extent in Khaptad. By themselves, Western trekkers are "green conscious," reflecting rising environmental concerns in their home countries. But every trekker or mountaineer in Nepal also brings along six porters to carry his food, fuel, and provisions. Armies of porters move through fragile Himalayan valleys like locusts, lopping off forests to keep warm.

At the end of every trekking season, the devastation is easy to see. On the steep flanks of the Barun Valley, the forests have been picked clean, and even the roots of the dwarf junipers have been yanked out as fuel for the base camps of expeditions.

With the roots gone, the moraine boulders are crumbling, making it a great hazard to traverse the trails. On the Ghorapani Pass on the Annapurna trek, the once-lush cloud forests are gone, replaced by gaunt skeletons of the majestic trees.

That was far from my mind as I guided the trekkers up and down the steep slopes of the Himalayas. Two decades passed before I realized I had not been back to Barpak Valley. My grandparents were dead, their holdings sold, and my father was in Chitwan. I felt better not revealing my identity. I sensed a distance, almost a hostility, among the inhabitants born and living in poverty. A man would not talk with his cousin because he feared that a story of misfortune would force him to share what little he had.

The Gurungs of Nepal have generally done better than Nepal's other hill tribes, like the Tamangs, Magars, Rais, and Limbus, because historically they had better access to Indian and British military recruitment. However, the hill folks of Barpak were slow to take advantage of this avenue. Being more remote than the Gurungs of lower down, they clung more stubbornly to traditional life-styles.

Padam Singh Ghaley (Gurung/Nepal)

Not having taken advantage of the good pickings of Gurkha re-cruitment, the Gurungs of Barpak today have become the slaves of development. A suspension bridge was built over the Daraundi Khola, and with it went all local initiative for bridge building. An irrigation canal is built, and with it goes the age-old arrangements of water sharing. If the crop is bad, the smart ones rush down to Gorkha to demand rations from the central district officer. There is agricultural credit, but Barpak residents do not get to take advantage of this facil-ity. The sharper villagers of lower down and the merchants from the trading posts manage to corner the development money and materials set aside for all of Gorkha district. The poor remain, largely, where they were.

There are jobs in road building and maintenance, there is primary education—but to what end? Is it any good awakening latent yearnings if there is no way to fulfill the new desires? I have no doubt that the people of Barpak are less happy than when I grew up there. This is because these days they are constantly reminded of what they do not have. While the villagers' lives are today where they were in the 1950s, in their minds they are poorer.

When the government nationalized the forests in 1959, the incen-tive to maintain the forests evaporated. The community's control or use of the forest was outlawed. It was now the district forest officer's worry. So as far as the villagers were concerned, it was now every man for himself.

But even so, the destruction of the forests in the Himalayas is not as big or as bad as the destruction of the villagers' self-confidence. Un-derstandably, the Kathmandu planners talk loud and long about land erosion, depleted forests (of the hills), and decreasing soil productivity. Radio Nepal carries these messages out across the hill communities. So the villager in Barpak today believes he is worse off than ever before.

While the official media have tried to convince the people how bad off they were, the development professionals have ensured that wherever development was tried, someone other than the target hill-people benefited.

You built a road, and the Sahus of the townships benefited from the cheaper transportation, not the hundreds of porters who relied on haulage for their only cash income. Trekking was supposedly a boon because of its purported ability to bring income directly to the villages, but the trekkers of my village brought in canned goods from Kathmandu instead of buying the local produce—not to mention what they managed to do to the environment.

At the base of Mount Manasalu and Himal Chuli lies Barpak. I have come a long way from Barpak. In fact, I no longer feel I belong to Barpak. But I do feel for the place, and its population, clansmen of mine who have been yanked out of their age-old life-styles and shown a vision of the world—a vision of the world that is not theirs.

RADHA BHATT

(Chipko/India)

Listen to the Voice of the Indian Himalayas

Radha Bhatt was born in 1934 in a remote village in Kumaon. She is a Gandhian and has been associated with Lakshmi Ashram in Kausaani in the Almora district since 1951. She worked with Sarla Behn, the English disciple of Mahatma Gandhi who set up the ashram, a self-supporting residential school for children, in Kausaani in the Kumaon Himalayas. Behn returned to Britain in 1966, leaving Bhatt in charge of the ashram, which she headed until 1989.

Since then she has been closely involved in the agitation to stop construction of the Tehri dam and in relief work among the survivors of the October 1991 earthquake in the Garhwal Himalayas.

Bhatt has traveled widely abroad on lecture tours or to attend seminars and conferences. A member of many Gandhian and activist institutions, she currently chairs the Himalaya Sevak Sangh. In September 1991, she received the prestigious Jamnalal Bajaj Award for her grassroots activism.

While writing this my heart and mind are full of scenes of the drama of destruction that was enacted in Uttarkashi, Tehri, and Chamoli districts at three o'clock on the morning of October 20, 1991.

After the earthquake, I saw villages where not a single house had remained whole. I saw people standing like broken trees after losing their children and other members of their families. I saw corpses of animals, and others in the last throes of death.

Was the earthquake not a slap on the face of a science that tries to win over nature? Instead of trying to conquer nature, we should live in harmony with it in the tradition of our forefathers.

In our culture, rivers are our mother. But in the modern tradition of science, rivers are to be harnessed. The villages high in the mountains in Uttarkashi district above the Maneribhali dam project were the ones most devastated by the earthquake. The blasting during the dam construction had probably weakened the mountains.

The village above Maneribhali dam is Jhamak, which was the most severely damaged village in the region. Maneribhali is not a big dam and is not producing very much electricity, but it was built some ten years ago using the same kind of technology as at Tehri, where construction on another controversial dam continues.

In building Maneribhali dam, rocks were dynamited and tunnels built, just like they are doing now in Tehri. Jhamak itself is on a tunnel. While the dam was being constructed, villagers told officials that they didn't want to live there because the village was in danger of collapsing if there was ever a calamity like an earthquake. They pleaded with the government to be shifted somewhere else. Activists were told then by the peasants that the dynamiting was making even the cattle restless, at night in their barns on the ground floors of village homes. The local people were clearly conscious of the danger.

As for the dam itself, the officials are not saying anything, even if the people supect that the tunnels dynamited out of the rock under the mountain during construction have been damaged by the earthquake. What they know for sure is that the dam gates were jammed after the earthquake.

Meanwhile, the construction of Tehri dam continues in this seismic zone because the officials have the arrogance of conquerors of nature. I have heard that attempts are being made to conceal the cracks in the dam. Local people, who are concerned about the danger, are prohibited from going to the dam site.

The Tehri dam has been controversial since the very beginning, and the local people have now told activists that they will support their fight against the dam. When complete, Tehri dam will be 260 meters high. At the time of this writing it is only 2 or 3 meters high, but if there is a crack being covered up, the dam will never be strong. Some scientists fear that if the Tehri dam collapses, it could, within twenty minutes, wipe out the temple towns of Rishikesh and Haridwar, less than fifty kilometers away.

This arrogance, which is called "development," is the biggest danger faced by nature, the environment, and the human race.

All the big Himalayan rivers—Pindar, Mandakini, Alaknanda—have hydroelectric projects on them, although none as big as Tehri.

The biggest problem for the local people is that the dams take away from them their most fertile lands along riverbeds. This affects the women most, because in the mountains it is the women who shoulder an extraordinarily high share of family labor, since men generally leave villages for jobs in the plains. In the mountains, agriculture and animal rearing are completely dependent on women. The women get their brightness and strength from working with nature, which also makes them independent.

In the course of my fifty years I have seen how the relationship between man and nature has deteriorated. For my grandmother and mother, the jungle was the most familiar, best-loved, and most rewarding work-place. Even if they were busy all day in the forests, they enjoyed themselves. Here I heard them sing, laugh with abandon, and share with their friends their innermost thoughts. They couldn't have opened up like this in their village and homes where they were tied down by societal responsibilities. That is why my mother and aunt preferred working in the forest to working at home.

All this left such a mark on their generation that I have heard my parents talk to the trees in the orchard: "Sorry I didn't notice your illness before. I'll take care of you."

This was not knowledge that came from scientific books and lectures. This was an awareness that grew within them as they passed a lifetime with trees, animals, air, water.

The seeds of this knowledge were passed on to me when I was ten. The first time I stood in front of an oak tree with a sickle in my hand to cut green leaves for our cows, my grandmother said, "Fold your hands in respect and tell the tree with humility: 'Oh God, forgive my hands and my feet for the sin they are about to do.'" Wounding the tree god with a sickle or even by climbing it was a sin in her view of life.

Anandbhai, a colleague from Sundarvarti village in Kumaon, tells a story from his childhood. His mother had a cow they called Godhan (cow of fortune), which was the family's source of happiness, good fortune, and peace. They did not believe in increasing the cow's productivity—stall-feeding to make the milk as rich as possible and later slaughtering the cow for meat. Anandbhai's mother was happy with the amount of milk Godhan gave the family. What was interesting was that the cow was like a member of the family. Anandbhai remembers that when Godhan slipped and hurt her leg during Diwali (the Hindu festival of lights), the family was so upset that no one felt like lighting even a single oil lamp.

Man is a part of nature and not its master. For a master, nature is a thing to be used. With seventeen people to a hectare, people in this region are hungry for farmland. But centralized development and industrial schemes like those in the mountainous areas of Bhimtal and Pithoragarh, and ugly monuments built to promote tourism, are taking away land.

In the mountains, farming is a woman's job. But peasant women in Bhimtal, in Nainital district, don't know what to do now that they have lost their fields and cattle, because, though the land is very fertile, the people sold it off to make Bhimtal an industrial township. Pithoragarh is the district headquarters, a township where offices now occupy what was previously farmland. The peasants sold the land and are now working in factories or in government offices. They are no longer independent farmers and proud of that tradition.

This kind of development, where you give no importance to farming or to ethnic groups and their cultures, is wrong. What you do is kill a community's culture. The gift of living in harmony with nature has given mountain women a deep understanding and maturity, which has been expressed in their lives and their protest campaigns. But today's development schemes that tamper with nature have changed women's life-styles.

In a study on mining in the Himalayas in Almora district, it was found that women living around the mountainous magnesite mines were unhappy because they no longer had cows and fields. Though they did not have to labor to cultivate farms and tend to cattle, the women all said they were scared of being cut off from their roots and losing the joys of living with nature.

This development, which is destroying their personalities, has also deprived them of their fundamental rights. Used to their own milk, butter, and honey, they now wait for milk powder, *dalda* (vegetable oil), and sugar from the plains. In this way, transnational companies have taken over people's lives. Is this development?

Development is when you make changes while respecting and

keeping alive all that is wonderful about traditional societies. But mistaken modern values have replaced peoples' pride in their society, respect for the environment, and desire for peace.

Man's craving for chairs and tables, paper, railway sleepers, resin, herbs, minerals, and wooden boxes for transporting fruit have left the forests naked. Mountain women can no longer beg the trees' forgiveness before cutting leaves like my grandmother and mother did. Today women are caught in a dilemma—they do not want to cut trees, but they need firewood and fodder for their cattle. What does a poor farmer do when she has to choose between trees or a hungry cow and a hungry child ?

Who is this scientific modern development for? Why is it only for people who have money? Why does it never profit ordinary people who are the majority? These questions have never been answered during the forty years I have been working, and they remain without answers. Women are the backbone of life in the mountains. A lot has been written about the heavy burden that women carry. But the new technologies have not lightened their loads. Women's problems instead have increased. Their burden has become heavier as they now walk greater distances to get water, fodder, and firewood.

The forests are now farther away from villages. Over the past few decades, natural streams and springs in the Himalayas have dried up as the forests disappeared. I will never forget the sight of women in Almora district carrying cans of water on their heads to irrigate distant fields. Most of the fertile land in the mountains has been taken over by dam projects and urbanization.

But in spite of this perverted development, women here continue to raise their voices in protest through popular women's movements—the agitation against liquor in the 1960s, the Chipko anti-felling campaign in the 1970s, the protest against mining.

The struggle against alcohol was the first time women had participated in a popular movement. The women protested that it is they
who suffer most if their husbands are alcoholics. They also said they
did not want development funded with money raised from selling
liquor, a large source of revenue for the government. They did not
want the government to make money selling liquor to their menfolk
to finance a handful of projects for people's welfare.

But it was the Chipko movement that brought the voice of the
Himalayas to the attention of the world. Even though the spokespersons in the Chipko movement are men, it was started by the women
in the Gahwal Himalayas, in a village called Reni in Chamoli district.
The villagers wanted permission to fell trees to make wooden ploughs.
They wanted to cut down the hardy ash tree or the oak tree. But they
were not allowed.

Soon after, however, the government gave permission to the
Allahabad-based Symonds Company, which makes sporting goods
like badminton rackets and hockey sticks, to cut five or six ash trees.
The villagers were very annoyed because officials clearly believed sports
equipment was more important than ploughs. This is what is wrong
with development—it is a case of getting priorities mixed up. People
can survive and eat only if they have ploughs. But officials give priority
to sports, not survival.

Naturally the people were very angry and decided not to allow the
lumbermen to cut the trees that they had lived close to for generations.
However, when the lumbermen came, the men were absent from the
village. They had been asked to go to Chamoli to collect long-overdue
compensation for land acquired by the government.

So the women decided to stop the lumbermen themselves. At first
they were laughed at, but the women fought back by standing in front
of the ash trees and telling the lumbermen: "The forest is our mother's

home. We won't allow you to cut the trees." They didn't hug the trees. They only stood in front of them and said: "If you try to cut the trees, you will first have to cut us down." In the evening, the workers were forced to leave.

This was the incident that gave birth to the Chipko Andolan (movement). News of what had happened in Reni spread slowly throughout the valleys into six or seven districts in the Gahwal Himalayas. People began to realize they could save their trees instead of just mutely watching them being felled and taken in trucks to the plains.

In Kumaon, a big forest had been given to the Star Paper Mills, which was permitted to cut stunted pine trees for which they paid a very nominal royalty to the government. But since no one was there to check, they were cutting down even healthy green trees. I can remember truckloads of logs going past my village to the plains.

When Chipko started in Gahwal, we in Kumaon knew that we could use the same method to stop forests from vanishing. The Uttar Pradesh government was told to cancel the Star Paper Mills contract. Though it took a long time—letters flew back and forth and there were several rounds of meetings—eventually the trucks were stopped from taking out logs, and the contract was canceled.

In the same way, in Tehri Gahwal, there was another agitation called Badyargarh, after the name of the village around which trees were being commercially logged and where, after a prolonged fight, the people were able to get the contract canceled. Another significant agitation was in Chamoli district's Paintoli village, where an oak forest was partly cleared to make way for a potato farm. The men supported the plan because they felt the farm would provide them with jobs, meaning they would not have to leave their village homes to look for employment in the plains. But the women did not think it an attractive project. They felt it was not wise to clear the oak forest because this would dry up their water supplies, and they would have to walk farther to collect their day's supplies of fodder and fuelwood. Chipko activists intervened, and after a while even the men came round to seeing the women's point of view.

In 1978, close to my ashram in Kausani in a village called Khirakot, the people began agitating against a mine sited in the nearby forest. Interestingly, the forest, which had become barren through over-exploitation, had only recently been greened thanks to the efforts of the village women who had agreed to refrain from collecting fodder, fuel, and green manure there.

But a soapstone mine-owner was permitted to set up mining operations. The women were angry; the men were not in the least bit worried. They even rebuked the women for not seeing that this was "development." A road would be cut to their remote village, and other modern facilities like electricity would also arrive, the men believed. The men also thought they would be employed in the mine. But, unfortunately for the mine-owner, two men died in the mine, and suddenly the villagers became wary. At the same time, the mine-owner decided to hire labor from the plains and migrants from Nepal. Lakshmi Ashram was invited to help the village peasants organize themselves to stop the mining, which was destroying their forest. After a two-and-a-half-year fight, the villagers won.

None of these protests have been easy fights. The people find themselves on one side, with the politicians, officials, contractors, and sometimes the media lined up on the other.

I have even been maligned as a woman with loose morals. But the people are very strong—and very united. They won, then planted trees where the mine had washed away the soil. This is how Chipko has grown, from stopping the cutting of green trees to stopping mining.

The main slogan of the movement is *"Kya hai jungle ke upkar—mitti, pani aur bayar"* (What does the forest give—soil, water, and fresh air).

We are against the Tehri dam because, though it will irrigate hundreds of acres of fields and produce electricity, it will take away from the mountain people more than it gives.

It is always said that a price has to be paid for development. But the question is: who pays the price? The answer is always: the poor. Why should those people who have lived in the mountains for generations, who have saved the forests and valleys through which the rivers flow, have to pay the price while outsiders who have money get the benefit?

Ironically, the Chipko movement is still fighting the same people who were timber contractors in the 1960s and 1970s, because when they were forced to stop cutting down trees they turned to mining. And while the small mine-owners are not the contractors building the dams—after all, they are not such rich people—we are fighting the same kind of people, the kind of people who think only about themselves. Development seems to benefit only these kinds of people.

Chipko is a movement for a sustainable life-style, the kind of life-style that the women of Reni, Paintoli, Badiyargarh, and Khirakot were all fighting for. The conflict is always between two life-styles—a life-style where money is the only thing that is important and a sustainable life-style that will save water, forests, vegetation, and soil for future generations. It is a life-style where people are independent, working with nature with no thought of conquering nature.

The key to this is letting the people themselves say what they want. We, the women of the Himalayas, have told the world clearly that our people will not provide the country with revenue from taxes on alcohol, but with air and a clean environment. Mountain rivers will not give the capital unlimited quantities of electricity, but will irrigate the fields in the Indian plains and make the soil fertile. Himalayan forests will not indiscriminately provide produce for consumerist cities, but will give the world a culture of peace and love.

Not only India but the whole world will have to understand and listen to this voice of the Himalayas.

Publisher's Note

Since the writing of this piece, work on the Tehri dam project has been suspended. Uncertainty over funding and a pending safety certificate from the government have placed in doubt the future of India's controversial dam project in the Himalayan foothills. While an expert panel set up by Prime Minister P. V. Narashimha Rao to examine the safety of the dam has submitted its report, Rao has yet to act on the secret report. Whatever his decision, work on the two-decade-old scheme has already been delayed by a cash crunch following the breakup of the former Soviet Union, a collaborator on the project; lack of funds could derail the project. The prime minister is thought to favor a liberal resettlement scheme for the more than 100,000 people being displaced by the dam.

The region was hit by an earthquake measuring 6.1 on the Richter scale in October, 1991, killing about a thousand people. The disaster bolstered the campaign against the project. In June Prime Minister Rao ordered a probe to look into the safety of the dam, after environmentalist Sunder Lal Bahuguna undertook a six-month-long sit-in and hunger strike at the site.

Environmentalists challenge the claim by the government that the dam blueprints were finalized only after taking into account the views of seismic experts, stating no rock-filled dam in the world has been tested for an earthquake registering 8.0 or more. Kellis Borok, a leading international seismologist from the former Soviet Union, expressed "grave doubts" about the dam's safety prior to the October quake.

The contractual responsibility for completing the dam rests with Russia, which is reportedly scouting for partners among international construction firms. Russian representatives told dam authorities that Russia will support the project only if a final environmental and safety clearance is obtained from the government.

KARAN SINGH

(Hindu/India)

Let No Enemy Ever Wish Us Ill: The Hindu Vision of the Environment

An activist in the environmental and global consciousness movements, the author of this essay has extensive knowledge of Sanskrit and the Indian cultural tradition. In 1981, Karan Singh spearheaded a new reform movement known as the Virat Hindu Samaj, which campaigned against the caste system's designation of "untouchable" and other customs that its members argued had weakened Hindu society for centuries.

Born heir-apparent (yuvaraj) to Maharaja Hari Singh and Maharani Tara Devi of Jammu and Kashmir, Karan Singh was eighteen years old in 1949, when his father appointed him regent on the advice of Indian Prime Minister Pandit Jawaharlal Nehru. In 1967, at the age of thirty-six, he became his country's youngest-ever central cabinet minister under Indira Gandhi. He has subsequently held various other government posts.

Karan Singh is a lifelong conservationist, having chaired the Indian Board of Wildlife for many years, and he headed the internationally known Project Tiger campaign that helped save the threatened animal from extinction.

Man is part of nature, linked by indissoluble spiritual and psychological bonds to the elements around him—this was the essence of ancient spiritual wisdom and is a distinctive characteristic of the Hindu tradition, the oldest living religion in the world.

The Vedas, those collections of hymns composed by great spiritual seers and thinkers that are the repository of Hindu wisdom, reflect the vibrancy of an all-encompassing world view that looks on all objects in the universe, living or nonliving, as being pervaded by the same spiritual power.

Hinduism believes in the overriding sovereignty of the divine, which manifests itself in a graded scale of evolution. The human race, though it may be at the top of the evolutionary pyramid, is not seen as being apart from the Earth and its multitudinous life-forms.

The Atharva Veda has a magnificent hymn to the Earth, comprising sixty-three verses redolent with ecological and environmental values, among which the following give an indication of the extraordinary depth of the hymn:

> Earth, in which lie the sea, the river, and other waters,
> in which food and cornfields have come to be,
> in which lives all that breathes and that moves,
> may she confer on us the finest of her yield.

> Earth, in which the waters, common to all,
> moving on all sides, flow unfailingly, day and night,
> may she pour on us milk in many streams,
> and endow us with luster.

> May those born of thee, O Earth,
> be for our welfare, free from sickness and waste.
> Wakeful through a long life, we shall become
> bearers of tribute to thee.

> Earth, my mother, set me securely with bliss
> in full accord with heaven,
> O wise one, uphold me in grace and splendor.
>
> Whatever I dig from thee, Earth,
> may that have quick growth again.
> O purifier, may men not injure thy vitals or thy heart.

Not only in the Vedas, but in later scriptures such as the Upanishads, the Puranas, and subsequent texts, the Hindu viewpoint on nature has been clearly enunciated.

It is permeated by a reverence for life and an awareness that the great forces of nature—the Earth, the sky, the air, the water, and fire—as well as various orders of life, including plants and trees, forests and animals, are all bound to each other within the great rhythms of nature.

The divine is not exterior to creation, but expresses itself through natural phenomena. Thus, in the Mundaka Upanishad, the divine is described as follows:

> Fire is his head, his eyes are the moon and the sun;
> the regions of space are his ears, his voice the revealed Veda;
> the wind is his breath, his heart is the entire universe;
> the Earth is his footstool, truly he is the inner soul of all.

In this view of the intrinsic relationship between the elements of life, animals have always received special care and consideration, and numerous Hindu texts tell us that all species should be treated as children.

In Hindu mythology and iconography, there is a close relationship between the various deities—who are all different aspects of the same divine power—and their animal or bird mounts. Each divinity is associated with a particular animal or bird, and this lends a special dimension to the animal kingdom.

In addition, as the Vaishnava tradition explains, the evolution of life on this planet is symbolized by a series of divine incarnations that begins with the fish, moves through amphibious forms and mammals, and culminates in human incarnations. This view clearly holds that man did not spring fully formed to dominate the lesser life-forms, but rather evolved out of these forms, is integrally linked to the whole of creation, and must necessarily revere animal life. The Yayurveda (13:47) lays down that "no person should kill animals helpful to all. Rather, by serving them, one should attain happiness."

This view was later developed by the great Jain Tirthankara, Lord Mahavira, who regenerated the ancient Jain faith that lives down to the present day. For the Jains, *ahimsa* (nonviolence) is the greatest good, and on no account should life be taken.

More recently, this philosophy was emphasized by Mahatma Gandhi, who always spoke of the importance of *ahimsa* and looked upon the cow as a symbol of the benign element in animal life. All this strengthens the attitude of reverence for life in every form, including animals and insects.

The natural environment also received close attention in ancient Hindu scriptures. Forests and groves were considered sacred, and flowering trees received special reverence. Just as various animals were associated with gods and goddesses, different trees and plants also had divine associations in the Hindu pantheon. The Mahabharata says "Even if there is only one tree full of flowers and fruits in a village, that place becames worthy of worship and respect." Various trees, fruits, and plants have special significance in Hindu rituals.

The Hindu tradition of reverence for nature and all forms of life, vegetable or animal, is a powerful tradition that needs to be nurtured again and reapplied in our contemporary context. India, whose population is more than 80 percent Hindu, has in recent years taken a special interest in conservation.

What is needed today is to remind ourselves that nature cannot be destroyed without mankind eventually being destroyed. With nuclear weapons representing the ultimate pollutant, threatening to convert this beautiful planet of ours into a scorched cinder unable to support even the most primitive life-forms, mankind is finally forced to face its self-created dilemma.

Centuries of rapacious exploitation of the environment have finally caught up with us, and a radically changed attitude toward nature is no longer voluntary, a question of acquiring spiritual merit or condescension, but of sheer survival.

As we enter the last decade of this extraordinary century—which has witnessed unparalleled destruction and unimagined progress; the cruelest mass killings in human history and the most outstanding breakthroughs in human welfare; the advent of weapons of unprecedented lethality and the creative probings into outer space—we find ourselves poised at a crucial crossroad in the long and tortuous history of the human race on Planet Earth.

In our own lifetimes, time has telescoped, both for better and for worse. While scientific applications have raised human living standards for millions beyond all expectations, the problems of humanity have also assumed global dimensions.

The persistence of nuclear testing and the disposal of nuclear wastes, the dangers of global warming and the breaking down of our ozone shield, the menace of deforestation and the destruction of many species of flora and fauna, the extensive air and water pollution and the poisoning of the food chain, the malign underworld of drugs and the alarming spread of communicable diseases—all these are now problems that the human race shares in common and that are simply not open to solution with anything less than a global basis.

At this crucial evolutionary crossroad, mankind is groping for a model, a new philosophy, a new paradigm, a new consciousness to replace the old. And it is no coincidence that this is happening at a time when the human race is in supreme peril: not from another species, not from outer space, but from itself. From deep within the human psyche, there has developed a terrible poison that threatens countless generations yet unborn; not only our own race, but all life on this planet. The dreadful Gulf War has sharply reminded us of the ecological disaster that will follow any major conflict.

Ancient myths often illuminate the human predicament, and there is a powerful Hindu myth of the churning of the Milky Ocean (the Samudra-Manthana) that speaks to us today across the millennia, symbolizing the long and tortuous evolution of consciousness on Planet Earth.

In this great myth, the Devas and the Asuras, the dark and the bright powers, both combined and cooperated in the churning of the ocean. This went on for eons until, at last, great gifts began to emerge: Kamadhenu, the all-giving cow, and Ucchaisharavasa, the divine horse; Kalpavriksha, the wish-fulfilling tree, and Airavata, the divine elephant. These and other great gifts appeared and were happily divided between the two sides. The churning continued, since its ultimate objective was the Amrita Kalasha, the pot of ambrosia, the elixir of immortality which even the gods crave.

Suddenly, without warning, the ocean started to boil with a deadly poison—the Garala—a new, malign dimension of which neither the Devas nor the Asuras had any knowledge. Rapidly the poison spread through the three worlds—the water, the land, and the skies. The churners fled helter-skelter in terror, trying to escape from the deadly fumes, forgetting all the gifts they had accumulated.

And then Shiva-Mahadeva appeared, the great, primal divinity who was aloof from the avarice and materialism of the Devas and the Asuras. He collected the poison in a cup and drank it, incorporating it into his being. His neck turned blue as a result, giving rise to one of his names: Neelkaantha, the blue-throated. Then the danger passed; order was restored. Chanting hymns to the glory of Shiva, the participants returned, and the churning was resumed until finally the ambrosial pot appeared and the whole process was successfully completed.

This myth vividly illustrates today's human predicament. Prolonged churnings have given man the great gifts of science and technology. There have been incredible breakthroughs in medicine and communications, agriculture and electronics, space travel, and cybernetics. We now have enough resources and adequate technology to ensure for every human being on Earth the necessary physical, intellectual, material, and spiritual benefits for a full and healthy life.

Yet, surely, the poison is also upon us. Billions of dollars and rubles, pounds and francs, are spent every day on the manufacture of monstrous weapons with unprecedented powers of destruction. It is estimated that there are now well over fifty thousand nuclear warheads on Planet Earth, each a thousand times more powerful than the bombs that devastated Hiroshima and Nagasaki at the dawn of the nuclear age, each with more explosive force than that used by both sides in the entire Second World War. And the Gulf War has demonstrated that despite the ending of the Cold War, regional conflicts can assume global dimensions.

It is now quite clear that humanity is making the transition into a new kind of society, a transition even more significant than the earlier ones from cave to the forest and from the forest to nomadic, pastoral, industrial, and then postindustrial society. What we are now witnessing, though we may be too close to fully grasp its significance, is the transition to a global society. The future is upon us almost before we realize that the past has disappeared, and we find ourselves precariously poised in a present full of challenge and change.

Whether it is political events or economic decisions, computer technology or space exploration, food and dress habits or the universal musical beat—all these have ceased to respect the artificial barriers imposed by national boundaries and have become global in their manifestation.

We live in a shrinking world, in which the old traditions of conflict and competition will have to make way for the new culture of convergence and cooperation if the rich promise of the next millennium is not to evaporate in a thermonuclear inferno. The ancient Hindu concept of Vasudhaiva Kutumbakam, the world as a family, is now becoming increasingly relevant to the human condition.

Among the many areas of prime concern today are the state of our natural environment and the role of the educational process in dealing with our present situation.

Enough has been written and said about the environment in recent years to show that we have paid a very high price for our economic growth in the last few decades. The multireligious Assisi Declarations on Man and Nature issued in 1986 are a valuable testament to the unity of approach to this crucial problem by spiritual leaders from many varied traditions, and the historic meetings of the Global Forum for Parliamentary and Religious Leaders in Oxford in 1988 and Moscow in 1990 further highlighted the growing awareness of the environmental threat.

Unprecedented human intervention in the environment has upset the delicate ecological balance that enabled Mother Earth—Bhavani Vasundhara in the Hindu tradition, Gaia in the Greek—to survive for billions of years and become a unique crucible for the evolution of consciousness.

Ruthless exploitation of nonrenewable natural resources has created havoc and, if allowed to continue, could result in a series of major ecological disasters that will drastically disrupt life on this planet. It is not that we lack the intellectual or economic resources to tackle the problems. Scientific breakthroughs and technological ingenuity have given us the capacity to overcome all these challenges. What is missing is the wisdom and compassion to do so.

Knowledge proliferates, but wisdom languishes. The yawning chasm between them will need to be bridged before the end of this decade if we are ever to reverse the present trend toward disaster, and it is here that education in the broadest sense of the term assumes such a vital position.

Unfortunately, all national educational systems are rooted in beliefs that flow from prenuclear and preglobal perceptions and, as a result, are quite unable to provide the new paradigm of thought that human welfare and survival now requires. Outmoded orthodoxies and obsolescent orientations continue to deprive the younger generations of an adequate awareness of the essential unity of the world into which they have been born. By fostering negative attitudes toward other groups or nations, these ideas hinder the growth of globalism.

Our astounding communications technology, which today encircles the globe, seldom uses its tremendous potential to spread global values and foster a more caring, compassionate consciousness. On the contrary, the media are full of violence and horror, of cruelty and carnage, which not only distorts the awareness of the young but dulls our sensitivity to the problems of human suffering and pain.

We urgently need a complete turnaround in our educational and communications policies. We need to develop carefully structured programs on a global scale, based clearly and unequivocally on the premise that human survival involves the growth of a creative and compassionate global consciousness.

Do we have the courage to think globally, to break away from traditional paradigms and plunge boldly into the unknown? Can we so order our inner and outer resources that we begin consciously to build a new world based on mutually assured welfare rather than mutually assured destruction? Can we, as global citizens committed to human survival and welfare, structure a worldwide program of education—for children and adults alike—that would open their eyes to the reality of the dawning global age and their hearts to the cry of the oppressed and the suffering?

If the answer to these questions is yes, as it must be, then there is no time to lose. As the ancient Chinese saying goes, it is later than you think. And let us not forget that along with the growth of global consciousness, the sinister forces of fundamentalism and fanaticism, of exploitation and intimidation, are also active.

We need a whole range of educational and teaching aids—films, audio and video cassettes, radio programs, and printed material—that are based on the following premises, which, though by no means exclusively Hindu, are based on the ancient wisdom and insight of this great tradition:

1. The planet we inhabit and of which we are all citizens—Planet Earth—is a single, living, pulsating entity; the human race, in the final analysis, is an interlocking extended family, Vasudhaiva Kutumbakam, as the Veda has it; and differences of race and religion, nationality and ideology, sex and sexual preference, economic and social status—though significant in themselves—must be viewed in the broader context of global unity.

2. The ecology of Planet Earth has to be preserved from mindless destruction and ruthless exploitation and enriched for the welfare of generations yet unborn.

3. Hatred and bigotry, fundamentalism and fanaticism, greed and

jealousy, whether among individuals, groups, or nations, are corrosive emotions that most be overcome as we move into the next century; love and compassion, caring and charity, friendship and cooperation are the elements that have to be encouraged as we move into our new global awareness.

4. The world's great religions must no longer war against each other for supremacy, but mutually cooperate for the welfare of the human race, and the golden thread of spiritual aspiration that binds them together must be nurtured, instead of the dogma and exclusivism that divide them.

5. The common people of this planet must urge and, if necessary, pressure their political and religious leaders into adopting postures in harmony with the emerging global society and shedding those based on outmoded and obsolete formulations.

As we produce such a package of educational material in all the languages of the world, let us simultaneously develop a delivery system that will ensure that it is in fact introduced in all countries. Agencies such as UNESCO and the United Nations University, national educational bodies and private educational organizations, will all have to be drawn into the complex process of incorporating the global dimension into existing educational programs.

The tremendous resources of the media will have to be creatively used if this whole project is ever to get off the ground. This is not some starry-eyed futuristic dream, but an absolute and urgent necessity if humanity in this nuclear age is to survive its own technological ingenuity and make a safe transition to a global society.

Ever since I first saw it, I have been fascinated by that amazing photograph taken from space showing our planet as it really is—a tiny speck of light and life, so beautiful and yet so fragile, ablaze with the fire of consciousness against the blackness of outer space.

Karan Singh (Hindu/India)

This Earth, looked upon in the Hindu tradition as the Mother, has nurtured consciousness up from the slime of the primaeval ocean billions of years ago to where we stand today. Now, in a dramatic reversal, it is WE who have to nurture this Earth, repair the scars that in our hubris we have inflicted upon her, and safeguard the welfare of all creatures that inhabit her today and will do so in the millennia to come. We are all children of Mother Earth and must repay the debt that we owe her.

As the Vedas sang thousands of years ago:

> May Earth on which men offer to the gods
> the sacrifice and decorous oblations,
> where dwells the human race on nourishment
> proper to the requirements of its nature—
> may this great Earth assure us life and breath,
> permitting us to come to ripe old age.
>
> Instill in us abundantly that fragrance,
> O Mother Earth, which emanates from you
> and from your plants and waters, that sweet perfume
> that all celestial beings do emit,
> and let no enemy ever wish us ill.

KING MOSHOESHOE II

(Basuto/Lesotho)

Return to Self-Reliance: Balancing the African Condition and the Environment

Environmental destruction is just one of the problems addressed by King Moshoeshoe II of Lesotho. He suggests that "in the search for solutions to today's rapidly increasing and interconnected global threats to the survival of all forms of life on our planet, much can be learned from comparing the dominant model of development—that of the industrial market society—with those traditional models" of the world's indigenous cultures.

The author defines culture as the sum total of original solutions that any group has found to adapt to its natural and social environment. These include all local knowledge, religion, customs, food and dress, language, values, socioeconomic and political behavior, methods of decision making, ways of exercising power, and methods of production.

In particular, King Moshoeshoe looks at what indigenous African culture understands by traditional beliefs, customs, ethics, and practices governing the human relationship with the natural and social environment, and suggests that self-reliance is the key to recovering culturally derived, sustainable, and locally understood means of progress.

Today Africans, like all the Earth's children, are born into a world with polluted air and water, into a world whose irreplaceable natural resources are rapidly disappearing.

They are born into a continent where many thousands die from starvation in a world where food is plentiful; a continent that, until recent times, was able to feed itself and produce surpluses, and where abject poverty was unknown; a continent where oppressive regimes, propped up by international finance institutions and local greedy elites, often deny basic human rights to their own people.

They are born into a world where technological advance now has the capacity to produce food for all and to provide each human being with the basic ability to seek and fulfill his or her own culturally defined well-being while preserving the natural environment.

Knowledge has been used to seek domination over nature, not to maintain the ecological balance, and to bolster an arms race that has used up vast quantities of the world's resources and many of the skills so urgently needed to meet the very basic needs of millions of the world's citizens.

Most of our global crises—war, pollution, overpopulation, overconsumption, hunger, and oppression—are symptoms of a single cultural evolution that is often referred to as "civilization." This is not to say that this culture—the Western evolutionist culture—has not shown brilliant success or offered much that is of value for the good of the rest of the world. But equally, careful study of other cultures, their forms of spirituality and ways of living in harmony with nature, could offer the West the seeds of a new relationship with nature, replacing the aggressive search for domination of nature and matter.

In the search for solutions to today's rapidly increasing and interconnected global threats to the survival of all forms of life on our planet, much can be learned from comparing the dominant model of development—that of the industrial market society—with those traditional models that sustained the indigenous cultures of Africa, Asia, and Latin America. As little as two hundred years ago, indigenous cultures, having evolved and successfully adapted to change over thousands of years, still occupied most of the world. But in these last two centuries, the culture of the industrial market society has become a global process, attempting—whether by seduction or coercion—to destroy all other existing cultural forms. In so doing, it has also created its own contradictions, giving humanity the power to extinguish not only itself but also many of the world's other species.

Outstripping human capacity to adapt in such a short space of time, the Western model of development, with its apparently inbuilt need to ensure access to and control of the world's resources, has drastically depleted these resources in a process of overconsumption. In Africa, as in the rest of the so-called Third World, the result has been ever-increasing levels of domination and dependence, socioeconomic decline, and a tragic loss of cultural identity. Once an integral part of African culture, life and survival skills—such as the ability to feed people, to provide a secure and stable community-based life, and to meet basic physical and emotional needs in a balanced relationship with the natural environment—have dwindled. These skills had been practiced over thousands of years, with no need for overconsumption, elaborate technology, centralized state structures, or the domination of the short-term material profit motive over nature.

The loss of such a way of life, and with it, of cultural identity, lies at the root of African underdevelopment and of the current African crisis—political instability, social and economic decline, poor governance, extensive corruption of power and privilege, and much else.

When a people lose their identity, they also lose their capacity for self-development, self-reliance, and self-determination. Society begins to disintegrate, and self-respect is replaced by alienation. Such is the experience of African culture in the face of colonization and neocolonialism. Having exploited and almost exhausted Africa's natural resources for over five hundred years, the West is only now awakening to the realities of the crisis in Africa. It has become more and more difficult for Africa's farmers to escape from, or to ignore, the agricultural and environmental dictates imposed on them by governments and their experts. But any intervention in the African environment is a much more serious undertaking for a subsistence economy than for Western society, whose industrial base acts as a safety net.

For the African farmer, conservation is a vital political and socioeconomic issue, a matter of survival. The management and ownership of land provide both livelihood and shelter. For indigenous African people, land has a mix of cultural and social meanings, in addition to its role as habitat and as a source of resources for production activities. In some African societies, land is related to lineage groupings, where boundary limits can be extended until an entire group is included in one single area, depending on the availability of unclaimed and unoccupied land, as is the case of the Tiv people of Nigeria.

There are also cases in which land is linked to social organization through a series of rallying points marked in a distinctive manner, as with the Tonga people of Zambia, who use what they called "rain shrines." Other people, like the Kikuyu of Kenya, had—and still have to some extent—a notion of territorial boundaries that could lead to the development of lineage estates or to units controlled by their management committees. In some parts of Africa, land was considered a national and social asset to be enjoyed by all with equal rights and obligations.

The central point is that land has always played a significant role in the indigenous culture of African people, and in their power systems and ideologies. It has always been a significant political and social issue, and it provided the basis for indigenous civilization, the molding of people's attitudes and behavior.

The environmental and agricultural dictates of Western solutions have seldom been instituted with the consent of, or in consultation with, local farmers and communities whose lives have been so vitally affected. "Experts" have shown a total disregard and ignorance of the African's long-established and successful methods to ensure their survival and well-being while safeguarding the soil, plants, and animals on which they have always depended for survival. Such "experts" have also failed to understand either the social or the ecological base of the cultural practices on which they seek to impose their externally derived solutions, constructed in an entirely different socioeconomic and ecological context. The result is that many of their agricultural strategies and environmental "solutions" have proved disastrous for the people, wildlife, and natural environment of Africa.

Indigenous cultures may not be able to replace modern political and socioeconomic analyses of world realities, but they can provide creative and innovative power to complement and correct current international thinking.

Environmental problems have always existed in all cultures and will continue to exist wherever there is an imbalance between the human population and its resource base. But today's environmental crisis is different in scale, being a global problem that has been caused by cultural forces unknown before the imposition of the modern industrial market society and its particular development model.

Before the arrival of slavery and colonization, African culture had its own structures of knowledge, values, religious beliefs, and social systems that ensured the protection of the natural environment. Africa was on course for progressive evolution, however differently the goals of that progress were defined from the progress of the Western development model.

African traditional belief regarded all natural resources as sacred and held in common and in trust both for those living and those yet to be born. In my own local culture of Lesotho, all land belongs to the nation—to the people as a collective whole. It is held in trust by the chieftainship system, whose member chiefs are responsible for its protection. Every citizen is entitled to a share of the land—for building a home, for pasture, for cultivation. These rights accrue on marriage, but single people are also entitled to land to build a home, independent of their parents' rights. In this way, the needs of the whole community are met—community good reigns supreme.

Traditionally, at the end of any growing season, all land was opened up to communal grazing, and the stalks of cereal crops had to be left in the ground for such grazing. No land was fenced. Other natural resources, such as trees, grasses, and reeds, were also communally owned. The woods were open only on certain days for the people to collect dead wood. Only the community could give permission for cutting other wood needed for building houses, and this permission had to be sought from the chief as the community's representative.

Traditionally, all local decision making is on a consensus basis, however long that process may take. Conflicts between individuals and offences against property are subject to community court procedures. The good of both parties is taken into consideration, in a search for solutions acceptable to all.

Within the priority of the good of the community, the dominant institution is the household—the extended family, comprising not only husband, wife, and children, but also brothers, sisters, parents, grandparents, and all other relatives, however remotely connected—in which individual duties to other members of the family are clearly defined.

The core household within the extended family is the basic production unit, creating its own economic system of satisfying material needs—the base of traditional African adaptive success. This mode of production is based on a division of labor, in which each member has a defined role, permitting the performance of all the technological functions involved in satisfying the needs of a family.

Wealth is traditionally measured in terms of the number of cattle owned. There is no limit to wealth, providing it does not challenge the stability and social cohesion of the community. If it does, the community reacts. The test would be whether an individual's accumulation led to undue envy, conflict, or fragmentation. Any community action would be seen as in the interests of its stability and coherence, and therefore legitimate.

Kinship also brings obligations on the wealthier to look after the needs of those who are less fortunate because of sickness, old age, lack of resources, or any other reason. Elderly people are respected because one day they will become the ancestors of the family.

Before the birth of the postcolonial African state, the preservation of equality was of central importance. The concept of social class as such was unknown. Status was a matter of age, sex, and personal qualities. Authority vested in chieftainship did not allow for personal aggrandizement. In African culture, the community could not shed its collective moral responsibility for the actions of the individual, and this in turn bound the individual to the religious and moral norms of the community.

In contrast, the Western idea of community is restricted to those living at any given time, without much sense of continuity between the past, the present, and the future.

In African traditional culture, there was a sacred bond between the individual, his community, his land, and the environment—the traditional source of African livelihood, of African culture, and of African thought. Such a bond engendered a collective moral responsibility for the present and the future. This sacred bond is only one aspect of African religion, which underpins all African thought and action and which is expressed in an ongoing and unending process of divine creativity—not only through nature but through each human being. In such a continuum, the individual is seen as a replica of the external universe, which is why it makes sense for each being to always seek harmony with the physical laws of the natural environment.

In this respect, Christianity and Islam have not been absorbed in total, but have been Africanized. Indigenous African religion has always believed in one god whose many aspects are reflected in the many aspects of nature. God is both within and without creation, present in all things as one all-pervading life force. It is not animism, as it is so often described, but a kind of pantheism where nature is seen as an essential part of a system of vital forces, which exist in equilibrium and which continually nourish nature.

In the traditional African world view, therefore, there exists an analogy between the behavior of matter and that of human society. The world is seen as a duality of matter and spirit, both in the person and in the natural environment—the spiritual being manifested through the physical. In short, two dimensions of the same divine creation.

In traditional African communities, everyone participated in all cultural activities and decisions and in this way achieved personal fulfillment. Poverty and alienation did not exist. The indigenous cultures of Africa developed their own science of social engineering, which aimed to satisfy, to reconcile, to harmonize, and to adjust all overlapping, and often conflicting, claims and demands in order to give stability to a society, clan, or other grouping. The ultimate objectives were to enhance social well-being, to promote economic growth for members of society, and to give pride of place to the individual's moral nature amidst the process of social change.

There was a conscious effort to improve living conditions—by creating new wealth and spreading existing wealth among all classes of society—so that the scourges of deprivation, marginalization, and poverty that endanger equality and cohesion would always be kept to a minimum. Indigenous traditional culture aimed to ensure that the physical surroundings—land, water, trees, grass, and other forms of vegetation—were conserved and developed to help all members equitably, protecting the poorer members. Indigenous culture was committed to social justice, social management, and the popular participation of all members, which in turn produced a fundamental cultural ethic of mutual assistance and cooperation.

In Africa, this culture fully understood what the environment was all about—a natural habitat in which the human being lives and interacts and on which it depends for survival. It was recognized that harmony between the human being and the environment is an essential requirement for any sustainable livelihood and development and that the overall balance and well-being of both the human being and the environment are vital. Within this world view, the human condition became a challenge, because the emphasis was placed on the dependence of human beings on the quality, protection, and conservation of the natural physical surroundings. This dependence constituted an essential link between the human being and the environment, and individual members of a community were called on to consider and decide upon actions for the protection and conservation of the surroundings.

Since the African concept of community covered not only those living at any particular time but also the dead (ancestors) and those yet to be born—in a process of community continuity that was seen as part of divine creation—African traditional culture had a fundamentally ecological nature, recognizing the equality of the needs of present and future generations.

Such a traditional concept required Africans to live in harmony with nature and so avoid any disturbance of the delicate balance between satisfying the needs of all equitably and conserving and protecting the resource base of the natural environment. Traditional communities knew immediately if their patterns of demand were creating any environmental damage. The traditional African economy operated on the principle that each person had an inalienable right to basic need fulfillment—food, shelter, clothing, education, and health care, as well as emotional and spiritual satisfaction.

This imperative took priority over profit making. Any attempt by one person to exceed certain limits of personal acquisition was seen as a threat to the stability of the community and discouraged by community disapproval. Isolation from community norms, and therefore from the community itself, was seen as emotionally and physically intolerable, devastating. Thus, when it came to the environment and protecting the needs of those yet to be born, the threat of community sanctions worked to put a brake on the destruction of too many trees.

With the introduction of external development strategies devised in the name of some external self-interest, alien monocultures were imposed on traditional communities and their modes of production, further impoverishing already fragile soils. Pressure was exerted on governments to enforce capital intensive technological cultivation of agricultural products for export, at the direct expense of production for local food needs, thus contributing to the present levels of malnutrition in Africa.

For example, the irrigation systems brought to the Sahel have caused a drastic change in the level of the water table and an increase in salinity. Instead of reversing desertification, such measures have only served to increase it. Large-scale project dams have put large areas under water, increasing waterborne diseases and reducing soil fertility.

The recommended use of expensive fertilizers and chemicals has increased the costs of food production and made many thousands of African farmers redundant, while increasing crop disease. Forests have also been uprooted in the name of increasing exports according to the needs of the Western markets, with catastrophic implications for Africa's ecological balance.

The strategies of Western development not only ignored African indigenous knowledge and expertise, but saw African culture merely as an obstruction to its goals, a barrier that had to be removed. This tragic failure to recognize the strength, the capacity of resistance, the durability, and the creative force of African culture is one of the main reasons for the abject failure of these externally derived strategies and structures. If African culture had been seen as the real and only creative base for change, the story might have been very different.

Instead, African culture faced no alternative but to surrender its capacity for self-reliance, self-sufficiency, and sustainable levels of consumption, a capacity that had existed before colonization. Such a surrender has opened the door to inequality, class divisions and conflicts, social and political instability, economic decline, and all the human deprivation that goes with the loss of African cultural identity.

Crude, repressive, and ruthless dictatorships have been consistently supported externally and so have reigned—in exchange for their compliance with the interests of the patron powers. Indeed, many of the African elites must share responsibility for this tragic sequence of events. Africans must not underestimate the degree of complicity of their ruling elites in acting to marginalize and sometimes even to repress their own African culture—for their own narrow power and privilege interests. In such a situation, those African leaders who wished to preserve their people's indigenous cultural paths to self-reliance and to socioeconomic progress through alternative development strategies found themselves isolated and under external threat.

By making it almost impossible for Africans to live outside the neocolonial system, Western development strategies—from colonization to the present day—have divorced Africans from their traditional ways of living in harmony with their natural environment. The collapse of the traditional system of local community control over its own destiny was what marked the beginning of Africa's current crisis of socioeconomic, cultural, and political decline. However, African resistance to acculturation from outside has always been there, and very many Africans have continued to live according to their traditional cultural values, proving how durable African culture will always be.

The Western economic model, seen as the panacea for world economic development, has stressed the relationship between human beings and material possessions—on the basis of competition—in stark contrast to the African emphasis on a socioeconomic order that regulates more equitable and harmonious relationships among people and between people and their natural environment. Modern Western political economy is based on the concept of the human being as *homo economicus,* someone who puts cost-profit analysis before anything else. Such a concept is alien to African thought.

The present African tragedy is, in my view, profoundly cultural and spiritual, rather than merely economic or technical. The attempt to destroy the African cultural base of daily living is at the heart of Africa's seeming inability to attain socioeconomic progress. It is not that Africans wish to return to the past as it was, but that Africans now know that they must have recourse to the past as an essential base for the future and for change, so that African culture may become the force for reconstructing African identity. Africa can then seek a cultural revolution that will enable and empower those changes necessary to meet Africa's own defined needs, within the world's realities.

Recognition of the African right to be different need not put an end to all forms of Western development. Africans can make constructive use of Western rationalism and expertise—just as long as they do not feel that their African identity is threatened or undermined in the process. Africans want to reacquire the right to decide for themselves what constitutes the "good life." The heart of the indigenous African culture's concept of self-reliance, all that constitutes their cultural identity, must become the basis for sustainable and ecologically sound African socioeconomic progress.

This is an environmental issue, in so far as self-reliance once again focuses economic activities on local needs and the careful sustainable use of local resources. Collective self-reliance has the ability to enable local autonomy, national self-determination, and self-development. But self-reliance itself depends on the existence of a nation's recourse to its own indigenous culture as its foundation, because it is the wisdom, skill, religion, and knowledge of the people that underpins their self-confidence in their own ability and in their own creativity.

Self-reliance is therefore an act of emancipation from all harmful forms of dependence—a fundamental factor in cultural identity and in the liberation of the African mind. Self-reliance erases excessive compartmentalism of the economic, political, social, and cultural spheres, uniting them into one culturally derived, sustainable, and locally understood means of progress.

Although Western-style economics and politics have acted to ignore the vital role of culture, a self-reliant culture must not ignore politics and economics. Africa does not deny the help and expertise of the West, but it wants to see this given on a more equitable basis of genuine partnership, in an alliance with the progressive forces of the North—a coming together in a joint effort to deal with the common problems of humanity, whose causes and manifestations cut across all borders and cultures, but which require the recognition that all peoples have the right to be different.

There is increasing evidence that many people in our world are recognizing this need for an alternative world order based on new concepts of what constitutes sustainable development for our common future and on a new mutual respect for the right to be different.

KAMORIONGO OLE AIMERRU NKONGONI
(AS TOLD TO LYNNE MANSURE
AND JONATHAN OLOLOSO)

(Maasai/Kenya)

The Circle Closes In on the Nomads

Kamoriongo Ole Aimerru Nkongoni was born about 1900. He has lived the life of a typical Maasai, serving as a warrior and a junior elder before becoming a senior elder. He is currently chairman of the Elders Meeting in his area. He lives with his four wives and a number of his children and grandchildren in a manyatta near Esonorua, a mile or so from the main tarmac road that joins Nairobi to Lake Magadi. (We did not ask the number of his children, as that would have been considered bad manners according to Maasai custom.)

Kamoriongo is widely respected in his area for his wisdom. But he considers himself "poor." His animals number only in the hundreds and not in the thousands as is the case for some of the Maasai.

At the beginning of the century, the Maasai ranged over a thousand kilometers of Kenya and Tanzania, from the eastern shores of Lake Taurkana in the north to what is now Dodoma in central Tanzania in the south.

With the advent of colonization, however, white settlers started to covet Maasai territory, and in the course of time it was decided to move the Maasai to the southern part of Kenya, which they now occupy. This area is divided into two districts: Narok, a largely high plateau area, and Kajiado, most of which lies at a lower altitude.

The Maasai currently number just over three hundred thousand.

171

Kamoriongo Ole Aimerru Nkongoni (Maasai/Kenya)

In his book Becoming Kenyans: Socio-Economic Transformation of the Pastoral Maasai *(Nairobi, Kenya: Acts Press, 1990), Dr. Mukhisa Kituyi estimates that the Maasai occupy nearly 7 percent of the total land area of Kenya, yet constitute only 1 percent of the Kenyan population. They have become "leading hosts to displaced peasants."*

This tendency to move landless peasants from elsewhere in Kenya to occupy parts of Maasailand was already under way during the colonial period. It was, however, cushioned by two factors. The first was the Maasai custom of integrating non-Maasai into their community. The second was that land rights, such as they were, were communal during the colonial period, so that immigrants who entered Maasailand came under the de facto jurisdiction of the Maasai themselves.

Things changed with the coming of independence in 1963. Gone was the idea of "reserves" for human beings. Any Kenyan could now live wherever he wished in the republic, and the gradual introduction of a modern system of land ownership meant that Maasai were now able to sell out to non-Maasai. The rate of this "invasion" of Maasailand by non-Maasai has been such that, according to the 1979 census, Maasai made up only 58.8 and 56 percent of Kajiado and Narok districts respectively.

Traditionally, the Maasai did not know the meaning of land ownership since they lived by a system of migration. So, before they came to know the value of owning land, many of them had already parted with it. Where, then, can they practice their pastoralism?

Deprived of a livelihood, will the proud Maasai end up as night watchmen in the suburbs of Nairobi?

Another factor that has had incalculable effects upon the Maasai has been the expropriation of vast tracts of their land for national parks, and, while it is true that the Maasai have coexisted peacefully with wildlife for centuries, it appears that wildlife can no longer coexist with the Maasai because, once a park is created, the Maasai are no longer allowed to graze there.

All in all, it is calculated that the Maasai today control only about one-quarter of the land they controlled at the beginning of the century. In addition, huge tracts of Narok district have now been given over to the growing of wheat. While this has put large sums of money in the pockets of the local Maasai, it has also led to environmental degradation, since the removal of grass cover in a fragile ecosystem leads to soil erosion.

With the best land having been taken over for agriculture or game parks, Maasai livestock are being increasingly pushed onto grazing land that is limited and marginal. In an effort to "modernize" the Maasai, the government has set up a system of group ranches in these drier areas.

Unfortunately, however, some members of these group ranches have taken the process of modernization one step further by subdividing their holdings into units that are, in any case, too small to be viable for ranching, and which, far too often, they end up selling to non-Maasai, thus disinheriting their sons.

Meanwhile, a major question mark hangs over efforts to "sedentarize" the Maasai, currently a declared policy of the government for which the very idea of nomadism is anathema. The well-reasoned logic behind Kamoriongo's justification for migration as being the best means of ensuring healthy livestock as well as protecting the environment merits more serious consideration.

—Lynne Mansure and Jonathan Ololoso

In the beginning, God was alone. His Maasai name was Ngai and he was omnipresent and self-reliant. Heaven and Earth were one, joined by water.

After a time, the water started sinking and Heaven and Earth parted. On top of the sinking water floated nests of all sizes, each containing a male and female of a different species. A little nest carried two safari ants, while a huge nest had two elephants. In yet another, there were two human beings, a boy and a girl. God provided food for all these creatures.

Gradually, the water disappeared. Some of it went to the south and some to the north. Mountains rose up and vegetation started growing. As the water sank, the nests came to rest on Earth and they broke, releasing the various animal species—lions, giraffes, flies, and, of course, human beings. All these creatures could speak and they all spoke the same language.

But then a problem arose—what to eat? In the beginning, they all ate fruit, but gradually some of them started to eat grass and some flesh.

It was then that God sent the cows down from Heaven on a ladder. They were sent to Maasinta, the first Maasai, who was told by God: "This is the last time I will do this for you, so you had better love these cattle the same way I love you." Ever since, the Maasai have been devoted to cattle.

The Maasai, a traditionally nomadic people of what is now East Africa, have stayed with their cattle and have loved them as instructed by God. They know that in order to remain healthy, cattle need enough grass and water, and that means continual migration to new pastures.

Today, however, land is no longer for everyone. Land has been sold off in lots, and if the Maasai no longer have grazing grounds, what will they do? A Maasai without cattle is no Maasai.

I belong to the Ilaiser clan of the Purko Maasai and my age-set is Ilterito. Like many traditional peoples of East Africa, the Maasai practice gerontocracy, the rule of old men, in which social promotion is based on a stratified system of age, with each age-set lasting about fifteen years.

Many members of the Ilterito age-set are now dead, but a few of us still survive. We are the ones who give permission for ceremonies like circumcision to be carried out; we help in cases where people have forgotten the proper ways to do things; we chair the meetings that decide general policies for the community; and we arbitrate in disputes or hand down judgment in criminal cases.

The group that follows us is called Linyangusi, and they are gradually taking over our duties because we are now old (I was born at the beginning of the century). The next age-set is called Eseuri, and this is the group the government prefers if it wants to appoint someone to a position of responsibility, like chief.

The youngest group of elders is called Ilkitoyiip. They are the ones who work the hardest since they are young and strong. They might be required to fight lions, drive the cattle long distances, or look for lost cows.

The cows are always at the center of the Maasai way of life. When God first sent down the cows to Maasinta, the women were jealous because the cows had more milk. One day, a woman was talking to a cow. She said, "My breasts do not have enough milk for my child." The cow replied: "You can milk two of mine but leave two for my calf."

Then the woman said, "My child needs meat," and the cow said, "Take a bow and arrow. Tie my neck with a rope and shoot the arrow at my vein. Take out my blood. It will clot and be like meat."

The woman said, "My child needs fat," to which the cow answered, "Put my milk in a gourd and let it become sour. Then shake it and you will have fat."

Finally, the woman said, "My child needs bone marrow." Replied the cow: "Now I see what your aim is. You want to bewitch me. Well, you can bewitch me if you want, but before you do I am going to tell you the four things that love me and the four that hate me.

"The four things that love me are man, who always defends me from wild animals; the rainy season, which gives me grass; moonlight;

and, lastly, a flat place. The four things that hate me are women, who cannot even bother to protect me; famine, which can bring about my death; darkness, where danger lurks; and the jungle, where wild animals abound.

"I have spoken," the cow concluded. "If you want to bewitch me now, you can."

So the woman went to the man and told him, "The cow is trying to curse our child. We must bewitch her." The man followed the woman's advice and bewitched the cow. From that moment on, the cow and all the other animals could no longer speak.

When God saw what had happened to the animals, he gave them the sense of smell so they could help protect themselves. Man was not given the sense of smell since God knew that if he had that sense as well as the ability to speak, he would have finished off everything on Earth.

After some time, there was a famine. The people were hungry and they started quarreling over food. God decided to create tribes. He gave each tribe wise men and a language and declared what food they should eat. The Kikuyu were given crops, and the Somali and the Maasai cows.

For the community to be prosperous, the animals have to get enough to eat, and this is why it is necessary to move around. In the past, a Maasai was able to go and establish his home wherever he wanted if no one was living there. If there was someone there, permission could be sought from that person or from the elders. Where the Maasai went depended on the seasons.

In the rainy season, you move far away from the rivers because animals can drink from pools. This means building different *manyatta* (fenced enclosures with huts and an open space in the middle where the cattle sleep). In the dry season, you have to stay near the rivers because the animals have to drink every other day, or, if the grass is in very short supply, every third day. This means that one or perhaps two days are for grazing and the third for going to the river. Donkeys accompany the cattle and bring back water for the people in the *manyattas*.

Generally, one should try to graze animals as far away from the rivers as possible. If the animals remain too near the rivers, the grass is destroyed. This explains why many *manyattas* are located far from the rivers, in the grasslands. This may be inconvenient for the people but it is better for the animals. It is also important that people live together in one place and that the rest of the area be left for the animals. If people live all over the place, there will not be enough space left for grazing.

I first came to live in the lowlands because it was good for the cows—there was a lot of grass and it was warm. I could not stand seeing my cows dying of tick fever up in the highlands. In those days, this place was good and I was alone here. Now, there are too many people and there is not enough grass. We have to send the cows back up into the hills to get enough to eat.

People stay too much in one place these days. They want to be near water, but the government also wants them to stay in one place. It says this area belongs to this clan and that area to that clan. Now, you can even find land belonging to an individual, which was never the case before. Even then, the Maasai allow others to graze on their land. If they do not, what will happen when they experience drought? They may need to graze on others' land then.

It is obvious that we have to help each other. In the old days, after a drought, if a person was fortunate enough to have had some of his own livestock survive, he was compelled to give some to kinsmen that had lost theirs. This is not so common today.

Cattle will always die off during a drought. That is why it is important to have many. A Maasai who has fewer than fifty cattle is a poor man. One of my age-mates has over two thousand and as a result is highly respected.

People need to be a part of a community, and for the Maasai this begins at circumcision, the first important event in the life of a young man. After he has been circumcised, the young man goes to stay with his fellow *moran* in the bush, facing dangers together. They hunt, become physically strong, and learn how to endure hardship without complaining. Most important, they become part of a group.

But things are changing. In the old days, warriors used to carry out cattle raids (on non-Maasais, naturally). These were acts of bravery, of courage, that took place in broad daylight. Nowadays, they go sneaking about and stealing at night. This is a disgrace to the Maasai.

In my days, the *moran* used to spend a full seven years in the bush. In that way, members of the age-set really got to know one another and to feel like members of a group. Now, with many of the young going to school, they spend much less time on their "*moran*ship" training. So the old discipline and feeling of group solidarity is bound to be less.

When the period of "*moran*ship" is finished, the *eunoto* ceremony is organized to introduce the young warrior as a full member of the community. He can then be given his inheritance by his father and have authority over his own cattle, goats, and other property. He can make his own arrangements for grazing them or even selling them. He may decide to set up his own *manyatta*, or if he continues to stay in his father's *manyatta*, he makes his own gate through which his property passes.

The next important step for a young man is to get married. He may take advice from his father or from his friends about a suitable girl, who must not be of his age-group or clan or be related to him. An ideal wife should come from a good family, one that is wealthy. She should be sociable, kind, hardworking, and tidy. If she likes cows and is good at counting animals, she will be an asset to her husband.

When the new bride arrives in her husband's *manyatta*, he allocates a number of animals she has to milk and take care of. In addition, each of the husband's immediate relatives will give her an animal, and from then on she will be known to these relatives by the gift they gave her. For example, the person who gave her a goat will refer to her as "owner of the goat," while the person who gave her a sheep will call her "owner of the sheep."

The husband will not allocate all his animals to his wife. He will retain some for himself, and should he wish to marry again, he will give the new wife animals from his own stock. It would be wrong to take an animal from one wife and give it to another. But the husband can sell or slaughter an animal he has already allocated to any of his wives.

A young man who has gone through the *eunoto* ceremony is considered a junior elder. He has the right to attend the elders' meetings. There are several types of meetings, those called by individuals to discuss a dispute, for example, and those to discuss general matters concerning the community, such as grazing arrangements or plans to move to another place. If bad grass needs to be burned just before the rains, a meeting will be called to appoint a junior elder to supervise the operation and make sure it is done properly so that trees are not destroyed.

Maasai learn to always treat members of their own age-set, and all other Maasai for that matter, as equals. That is why the Maasai hate the idea of being employed. Each man should depend on his own property. Of course, there are always some people who are poor. In such cases, it is better to ask such a man to look after your animals, and after some time, you give him a gift of a cow or a goat. In this way, he will get his own property, and eventually he will no longer be poor.

Nowadays, everything is different. When I was young, there was a lot of rain. The rivers used to overflow; now the weather is changing. Sometimes I wonder if God is not punishing us for our sins, but only he knows the answer to that. We believe many of these problems have been brought to us by outsiders (people of other tribes). As Maasai, we are not allowed to cut trees or bushes on the riverbanks. Some outsiders divert streams into their properties for irrigation. The Maasai believe this is why streams and swamps are drying up now. It is bad to break the soil and destroy the vegetation that could otherwise support a number of livestock.

It is becoming more and more difficult to move from one place to another for grazing, because people have been given certain pieces of land, and some have been allocated a dry area, meaning they will be forced to depend on those who have been given a good area. For the Maasai, it is important to have one *manyatta* for the dry season and another for the wet season. How can this be possible if each person has only one piece of land? The animals might have to travel long distances to get good grass, and they will be tired. At the same time, if they end up staying in the same place, pastures will not recover and the animals will be weak. This is what is happening now. Animals are weak, and they don't give much milk. As a result, children suffer.

Some of the places where we used to take our animals have now been made national parks, and we are not supposed to go there any more. This is unfair. We should be allowed to take our animals there, at least during the dry season. The Maasai do not bother the wild animals, we leave them in peace because they are part of God's creation.

When I was young, the land used to belong to everyone, but now some people have title deeds, and then they start selling the land, sometimes for very little money. Some of those who have sold their land are grazing their animals on the land that belongs to other people or that belongs to the government, some are working for others, all of which is bad for the Maasai.

What I have seen is that, nowadays, people do not respect one another as they used to do. They have become greedy and they think only about money. Some have become very rich while their kinsmen and age-mates remain poor. Instead of helping each other as they should, they look after themselves.

I have seen all these bad things, but what I know is that the Maasai were given the rules of upright conduct and social organization by Maasinta, the first Maasai. He is the one who named all the plants and animals and who gave us our proverbs. Whatever happens we should continue to follow what he taught us.

Not only that, the Maasai should continue to respect their elders. We have a proverb that says, "The neck cannot go above the head," meaning that those who are older need to be above the younger people.

In the end, a Maasai without cattle is no Maasai. He is powerless and is not respected by society. We have to continue to live with our animals because that is the life we know. Cattle were given to us by God, so we must continue looking after them in accordance with his will.

BAHER KAMAL

(Nubian/Egypt)

The Nubians: They Built a Dam to Take Away Our River

This chapter is a synthesis of accounts collected by the Egyptian journalist Baher Kamal and narrated by members of a Nubian community living in Kom Ombo, southern Egypt, who were displaced from their lands in the 1960s as a result of the construction of the Aswân High Dam.

For the Nubians, and long before Western travelers came to document it, the Nile has always been the beginning and end of all things. According to the mythology of our ancestors, the world was born of the chaos that resulted from the dramatic arrival of the first waters of the river to our lands.

It was on the basis of this concept that our people developed the idea of a spiritual relationship with the universe, turning into cults the four fundamental elements: *nun* (water), *geb* (earth), *shu* (air), and *atum*, or much later *ra*, which represented the sun and, in a way, also fire.

Such a view was shared by the Nubian and Egyptian peoples, who, during the predynastic era (that is to say before the year 3200 B.C.), were not only one homogeneous people but, above all, shared a common culture.

But with the passing of time, and already halfway through the third millennium B.C., Nubians and Egyptians had begun to drift apart in terms of customs and traditions. The Egyptians conceived the principle of the social structure of the modern state, while the Nubians continued immersed in their primitive cultural forms.

The Nubian culture developed over the millennia and throughout the extent of our lands, which, according to Nubian scholars, covered one-third of present-day Egypt, the whole of Sudan, and parts of Ethiopia, always flanking both banks of the Nile. In a word, our culture centered almost exclusively on the Nile, and the annual rise in the level of its water was a constant source of joy and fear. Joy, because the lime carried in its waters was a natural fertilizer for our soil and helped ensure the growth of abundant crops using simple forms of agriculture. It was enough to be in harmony with the cycles of the Nile; fear, because on occasion the rise of the river was such that land and houses were flooded.

This is why we developed the tradition of making offerings to the Nile, giving gifts to the spirits of the river in the form of baskets of food, seeds, and beautiful primitive handmade objects to ask for bounty and chase away the ghosts of destruction.

This culture and way of life survived even the military campaigns mounted by the Egyptians against our lands starting around 2000 B.C. and the annexation of a sizeable portion of our country, stretching over today's Edfu and areas of northern Sudan.

We Nubians eventually came to govern Egypt under the twenty-fifth dynasty, with five pharaohs overseeing the destiny of the country in the period 747–656 B.C. From then on, the world witnessed a series of major historical developments, but none created deep change in the life of our people. For example, in the seventh century A.D., the Roman pharaohs in Egypt obliged the Nubians to adopt Christianity as their religion. Nevertheless, the new forms of worship did not radically replace either our beliefs or the religious rituals that continued to be centered on the waters of the Nile.

Baptism took the form of direct immersion in the waters of the Nile, as did a form of first communion. Spouses-to-be were blessed and purified with the waters of the Nile. The dead received the blessing of the river with the sprinkling of the water of the Nile over their tombs.

Subsequently, five centuries ago, the Nubian people were subjected to another change brought about by the imposition of Islam as the official religion. Even then, and despite the change, families that had been Islamized continued their traditional religious ceremonies and rituals, in a surprising mix of the ancient, the Christian, and the Moslem.

The constant thread that ran through these changes and historical developments was the Nile. The soil bathed by its water provided us with food. This same land straddling both banks of the river supplied us with the material to build our houses and create villages at a safe distance and height in case of the extra strong swelling of the waters of the river.

The walls of the houses were decorated with brightly colored paintings that depicted the most important scenes of everyday life, in particular scenes of happiness and abundance, like bountiful palm trees, weddings, and, starting with the period of Islam, commemorations of pilgrimages to Mecca.

Life went on without dramatic change right up to the start of the twentieth century, up to the moment when the first dam was built at Aswân in 1902 to control the flow of the waters of the Nile and ensure adequate levels of water throughout most of the year. It was then that the Nubians suffered what can be called the first-ever operation of forced mass migration. Before the dam was built, people were forced to move from time to time because of natural elements, such as the rise in the level of the Nile—but always because of factors far removed from the activities or control of man. With the building of the dam, we lost one-third of our land.

Work carried out in 1912 and 1933 to raise the height of the dam brought about further displacement and the loss of another third of our land, leading to the parallel phenomenon of an increase in the migration of Nubians toward the major urban centers of Egypt, above all Cairo.

Before the building of the dam and the work to increase its height, if Nubians emigrated they did so for only a few years, always returning to their villages and settling back into their previous way of life. All that changed with the arrival of the dam, as the number of Nubian migrants increased and they began to stay away for ever longer periods of time.

This produced a dramatic transformation in social and traditional structures. Even today, there is the widespread view circulating among the elders of our people that if it had not been for the dam at Aswân, no Nubian youth would have left the village to emigrate to the city.

In the final analysis, however, the most profound change in our way of life took place in the 1960s with the construction of the Aswân High Dam (a mass of concrete and iron measuring some 43 million cubic meters in volume and built with enough material to have constructed seventeen pyramids the size of the Cheops pyramid) and Lake Nasser, which, with a surface area of 225 square kilometers, is Africa's largest artificial reservoir and one of the biggest in the world.

On this occasion, the voice of alarm rang in all four corners of the world: the huge operation of modern engineering was about to bury forever under the waters of an artificial lake a host of impressive architectural masterpieces, witnesses to the glory of the Egypt of the pharaohs. To rescue them, an authentic worldwide alliance was created, and twenty-two countries, along with international organizations, mobilized all their technical knowledge and immense sums of money to save magnificent works of art, such as the Abu Simbel temples, for example.

Despite the effort, little was said or written about the fate that lay in front of the Nubians, the people on whose land the monuments had been built and whose houses were destined to disappear forever under the waters of the lake. It is true that the governments of Egypt and Sudan (the dam and the lake also affected our brothers in the northern part of the neighboring country) drew up plans to relocate the displaced Nubians (more than fifty thousand in Egypt alone starting in the 1960s and as many again in Sudan) in new settlements scheduled to be built in such a way as to reproduce, as far as possible, our traditional villages.

But it is no less true that the forced displacement of Nubians in Egypt and Sudan meant far more than just a change of dwelling for us Nubians: it was above all a hard blow to our millenarian culture and traditions. Related problems aside, such as the fact that thirty years later on some houses and plots of land still have not been assigned to those displaced earlier, our direct contact with the Nile—and this is the crux of the issue—has been definitively altered. Today, in the new houses, water arrives through tubes. The area that houses our displaced people in Egypt, in Kom Ombo, some fifty kilometers north of Aswân and more than two hundred kilometers distant from our former settlements, is called New Nubia. But it does not offer the same living conditions that we used to have.

Some houses are situated right on the edge of the desert, at least ten kilometers away from the river. The soil is arid and infertile. To cap it all, we are deprived of the fertile lime washed ashore when the waters of the Nile rise. Our farmers and fisherfolk, along with many other Nubian men and women, have had to move to the cities to find work as house servants or waiters and porters. Not even projects to rehabilitate the land alongside the artificial lake, nor the often conditional concessions granted to Nubian fisherfolk, have been effective mostly because of bureaucratic red tape.

At the same time, our new houses are much smaller than those that our people were used to. In the past houses were much more than simple dwellings; they were the center for the extended family.

To give one example of our ancient traditions: the family of a young recently married woman opened up their home to the new husband for a period that could last up to two years. This tradition fulfilled two functions: to accustom the husband to the ways of the wife's family and to help the husband save money to build a house nearby. This is no longer possible because the houses are so much smaller and don't have the extra space for a married couple.

Previously, the population density per house was 0.7 persons; today it is 1.6. That means that each of us now lives and dies in not quite half the space we had before.

It also has to be remembered that previously our people in Egypt were scattered throughout some six hundred villages; today, we are down to just forty-three. In Sudan, where the artificial lake also flooded the land of the Nubians, the same phenomenon occurred, with the additional problem that the fifty thousand people affected were transferred to Khashm el-Girba, some six hundred kilometers away from their ancestral lands.

The land that has been assigned to the Nubian people in the new settlements lacks quality, is often insufficient, and is often far from living areas. And that's not all. We have even been forced to start different forms of agriculture, like growing sugarcane, which, according to the government, should cover 40 percent of the surface area of our land allotments.

Even more, the water rationed to us for irrigation no longer contains the lime carried by the Nile, meaning that we now have to use chemical fertilizers that we know nothing about. This is not good either for the soil or the crops or the health of the people, who often don't know how to use these new fertilizers.

On the other hand, the heavy migration of menfolk, due to the scarcity of land in the new settlements for traditional crops and the change in patterns of traditional sources of survival, has meant that they have acquired new urban customs and ways, many of them Western, and that they have married non-Nubian women.

This has contributed to the disintegration of our nuclear family—one of the pillars of our culture, where the family was the entire village.

The elders tell us now of how the new situation has produced customs that were nonexistent before. In the old days, families or villages exchanged food through barter. Payment was made with dates. Today, everything is bought and sold. Our fathers and grandfathers ate what they produced on the land. Today, you have to go to shops to buy different food products, each of which has to be paid for in cash.

Meanwhile, the worldwide campaign to save the monuments of the land of the Nubians has given birth to mass tourism, which in turn has either attracted or obliged our young people to move into the service sector at the expense of agriculture or fishing. The contact with foreigners has also led to the superimposition of Western customs onto our traditions.

One example of a change that may seem trivial, to show how it affects us: in wedding ceremonies, the people of the village used to get together to greet the new spouses with dances and songs that recounted the history of our forebears. Since the villagers themselves were the protagonists of the festivities, this helped reinforce the ties between them and the new nuclear family. Nowadays, wedding feasts are increasingly celebrated to the sound of electronic music, which is impersonal and often foreign. The presence of friends and relatives has been reduced to little more than a mere ritual.

Even if the sum of the negative effects on the environment of the construction of the dam and the artificial lake has not been quantified, our elders believe that the drought that has affected the region of the Nile for the last nine years is directly due to this construction, which changed the flow and life of the river.

In this sense, what some technical experts say is true: that with the construction of the High Dam, the Nile has been broken off at Aswân. From there to its mouth in the Mediterranean, the Nile has been transformed into a virtual canal.

None of this is a question of simple nostalgia for the past. One of the most serious problems was the loss of the lime that fertilized our soil in a natural way. Now, it is all blocked behind the dam. What we get now is just water, not a natural gift. But the lime was useful not just for fertilizing the soil. Many Nubians worked in the almost seven thousand small factories that used lime to create building material. Now they are unemployed, even twenty years after the promise of building a new factory. This loss has created other problems, for example in sardine fishing, because the once abundant sardines fed on lime.

It is true that, with the passing of time, fish production has grown thanks to Lake Nasser. But it is no less true that there has been a fall in the availability of the type of food we were once used to and that the people who lived from sardine fishing and small family industry have suffered a major economic and social setback.

One further problem caused by the lack of lime is the heavy deterioration of the banks of the Nile, and even the coastline to the north. If the rise in the level of the river used to mean the flooding of the land, at the same time it left behind deposits of lime. There was a natural balance. This is no longer the case. Now the soil suffers from erosion, and not only along the banks of the Nile. The delta lands to the north of Egypt are now much more exposed to the waters of the Mediterranean because of the disappearance of the lime, which formed a sort of barrier as well as being a source of natural fertility.

The problems don't end here. There is also the fact that, with the huge quantity of liquid amassed in the reservoir and the lack of adequate drainage systems, the level of subterranean water has risen dramatically and dangerously. Technical experts agree that this level has risen from an average of fifteen meters below ground level to around just three metres today. In Cairo, it is estimated that underground water is now at a depth of less than one meter in some parts.

Monuments are directly affected because the underground water has reached the level of their foundations. Remember the Temple of Karnak, in Luxor, where the foundations were affected by previously nonexistent damp. The interior of the Temple of Nefertiti is more affected by the dam than the exterior. And the Sphinx runs the same risk. These are just a few examples.

Another serious problem is the evaporation of the waters of the river, due to the enormous surface area of the reservoir exposed to the rays of the sun. Some experts have estimated that 50 percent of the water collected and stored in the reservoir is lost through evaporation. And while some of this loss is compensated for by heavier rains in the area of the reservoir, it remains true that the climate has changed.

This is not to suggest that the High Dam and the reservoir have not brought benefits. Nor that no attempt has been made to solve many of the problems created. Even less to say that our people are against the development of Egypt, a country with which we have identified ourselves for a large part of our history. But the price we have paid and continue to pay is very high. Above all else, we have lost our identity, the identity of a people that has contributed much to the history of this country.

Despite all this, we Nubians are doing what we can to safeguard our traditions. Unfortunately, we have to do this using modern structures. To help maintain contact among the million Nubians that are estimated to live in Egypt (another million live in Sudan), forty-three associations have been created. These associations, which have their headquarters in the principal cities to which Nubians have migrated (Cairo, Alexandria, Ismailia, and so on), are grouped in the General Club of Nubians, based in the Egyptian capital.

These associations are meeting places for Nubians, places where they celebrate weddings in those cases—increasingly more frequent—when they cannot do so in their villages; where communal vigils are organized on the death of a Nubian by his or her people; where collections are organized to help the neediest; where news is exchanged, songs are sung, and folklore evenings are held. And the people can speak in their own dialects. This is of extreme importance for the conservation of the Nubian languages—no longer written but still spoken.

We are making an effort to revive some of the traditions of our ancestors, even if we are far away from the lands of these ancestors—lands that are now irreversibly under water—and far from our families, who have been torn apart.

The Nubians, even if they are not looking for separation or independence from Egypt and Sudan, where they live and work, are living a sort of exile.

This is the price that our people—who have given much to Egypt, who developed our own formidable culture, who once knew abundant harvests and practiced fishing but now serve as waiters in the big cities—have had to pay for a modern technology that has tried to domesticate the Nile, their Nile, and to generate electric energy to ensure that the TV sets of today can show neverending hours of foreign soap operas and game shows.

PEKKA AIKIO

(Sami/Finland)

Beyond the Last Line of Forest Trees

Pekka Aikio, a member of the Sami people, heads a research program on Northern indigenous cultures and reindeer herding at the Research Institute of Northern Finland at the University of Oulu. A Sami politician for the last twenty years, he is currently vice-president of the Finnish Sami Parliament and chairs the board of the Nordic Sami Institute.

The cloud of radioactive fallout that passed over Scandinavia following the Chernobyl nuclear disaster of 1986 was just the latest in a series of events that have progressively been damaging the natural environment of the reindeer herders of Sapmi (Lapland), the home of the Sami people. Forest clear-cutting, construction of reservoirs, mass tourism, and already excessive levels of air pollution had already dealt a harsh blow to the Samis, an indigenous people who had learned, like the North American Indians and the Inuits (Eskimos), to adapt themselves to the harsh environmental conditions of life in the Arctic circle.

In the northern sub-Arctic and Arctic regions, the adjustment of human behavior to the "economy" of nature has always been a challenging endeavor, where practicable alternatives are few. But the indigenous people inhabiting the northern circumpolar areas had always managed to adapt themselves to their surrounding ecosystem, and their success in survival—today under serious threat—could be a useful indication to biologists of how to keep the marginal areas of the Earth inhabited by humans.

Traditional Sami culture was based on the subsistence economy, an economy that was almost entirely self-sufficient, dependent on fishing, hunting, and reindeer herding and geared to the surrounding ecosystem, using natural resources in an ecologically sustainable manner. The aim was long-term well-being, using large tracts of land gently, one section at a time.

The Sami of today recognize that because their environment is so sensitive it will be impossible to rectify any damage for centuries, if ever. Through colonization, they argue, the surrounding society has influenced the environment and their economic activities, gradually taking away from them their land and water.

For the Sami, man is part of the ecosystem, with society adapting to an ecological balance between what nature can give and what man can use. The Sami people, like their indigenous sisters and brothers, say: "The Sun is our father, the Earth is our mother." Tradition teaches the Sami how nature is to be used without being consumed. The Sami culture is a living culture that enables the people to adapt to various natural conditions and to acquire new knowledge that will enable them to survive. The social environment—relations between individuals or within a group—can easily respond to changes, both in the natural environment and in the culture. The social environment is always characterized by the attitudes we have toward nature.

Our traditional forms of economic activity have always been based on a holistic view of the world and structured on a self-regulating basis. If production of a particular resource becomes impossible at a certain time, an alternative is found until the original resource has recovered. This self-regulation is built into our economic structure through the combination of traditional and modern economic activities.

The Arctic is an exceedingly sparsely populated region (though one could call it the most densely inhabited "wilderness") of the world, totaling only a few million people. But there are over seventy circumpolar indigenous peoples, of whom the Sami people form a relatively uniform group.

The Sami presently form communities in Finland, Norway, Sweden, and the Soviet Union. The area inhabited by the Samis encompasses a crescent-shaped zone extending from the eastern edge of the Kola Peninsula in the Soviet Union and running along the northern periphery of Fennoscandia (Finland and the rest of the Scandinavian peninsula) to Dalarna in Sweden and Roeros in Norway. The Sami represent the oldest known population of the area, dating from prehistoric times.

For centuries, the Sami people had been able to live on the fringes of the polar ecosystem, an area beyond the last line of forest trees, where agriculture is unable to provide the basis for self-sufficiency, mainly because of the severe natural conditions. The Arctic climate is harsh, and though vegetation is surprisingly varied, with lichens, mosses, and herbaceous plants the most common, the fauna is relatively limited. Typical land animals include the musk-ox, polar bear, wild reindeer, arctic fox, wolverine, lemming, and stoat.

On the other hand, the Arctic supports a vast aquatic fauna, partly a consequence of the relatively plentiful supplies of plankton and partly a result of the migratory habits of many fish species that are only partially dependent on the food supplies available in the area. The major species are whales and seals, walrus, cod, and a variety of fish related to the salmon family.

It is clear that the relatively limited vegetable and animal resources of the area can sustain only an extremely sparse human settlement pattern. However, the modern technological culture that has spread to the area in more recent times has led to a sharp increase in population and settlement centers.

Those dependent on hunting, fishing, or reindeer herding for their livelihoods were nomadic peoples, moving in groups whose size was determined according to the organization of these activities. Over the centuries, the seasonal fluctuations in ecological conditions and availability of natural resources have led to the creation of powerful forms of social organization.

The length of the Arctic winter makes it difficult to keep livestock, and cereal plants do not grow. At the same time, the territory occupied by the Sami of Fennoscandia is extremely small compared with the areas inhabited by the Indians and Inuit of North America, who were able to continue their hunting culture within traditional territories undisturbed up to modern times. For this reason the Sami faced the limited scope of their natural economy at a very early stage.

As a result, they adapted themselves to the external conditions by creating a culture based on reindeer herding within which it was possible to practice a certain type of animal husbandry without the necessity for indoor animal feeding. In this way, the level of intensity of economic activity could be increased without ecological damage. The equal and complementary relationship between man and reindeer was the basis of an entirely original form of social and economic organization and as far as the stabilization of their means of livelihood was concerned, one of the greatest achievements of the peoples of the polar regions. Up until the introduction of modern mechanized methods of herding, this economic activity functioned well with a minimum of investment of resources. Today, out of a world total of 4.5

million reindeer, 3 million are domesticated, 77 percent of them in the Soviet Union and 21 percent in Finland, Sweden, and Norway. Though there is little information on reindeer herding in ancient times, there is some evidence that reindeer herding is one of the oldest forms of human economic activity in the northern polar region.

In the early 1970s, in the southwest corner of Finnish Lapland, near the city of Tornio, a piece of a reindeer horn was found that was estimated to be thirty-four thousand years old. There are also many rock drawings—including the famous ones in the city of Alta in northern Norway that are more than five thousand years old—drawings that depict the form of a four-leafed clover, inside which are reindeer, elk, men, plus shapes resembling boats or sleds.

The reindeer used by the Sami were tamed from the wild mountain reindeer, but not merely to transform them into mechanical domestic or purely utilitarian animals. The process was one of "biological mutuality," in which man used reindeer for food, clothing, means of transport, and so on, without endangering the functions of the ecosystem, while the reindeer got help from man in adapting to new ecological circumstances, primarily the danger of predatory animals in the forest zones, the continuous use of shifting grazing grounds in an area with small basic production, and many physical conditions that changed according to the seasons.

Against this background, some sixty regional reindeer-herding associations have been established this century, one of them being the Lapin Paliskunta, managed by the Sami in Finnish Lapland. But over the past thirty years, great technological and economic changes have affected reindeer herding, transforming it from an activity closely identified with the ecosystem in which it operated to one detached from that ecosystem. This has been accompanied by rapid and complex social changes that have affected Sami communities.

The economic expansion of the state of Finland resulted in the building of the man-made lakes of Lokka and Porttipahta in the 1960s. Their construction was preceded by the removal of trees in the basin beginning in the 1950s; at some points the completely cleared area even extended beyond the shoreline of the basin. Large forests were also felled outside the basin area, and deciduous trees were similarly destroyed by spraying herbicides from airplanes. Today, the reindeer grazing grounds are not homogeneous. Through the loss of land, some vitally important winter grazing grounds were erased, and increased pressure came to be exerted on other grazing areas. The result has been chaos.

The felled and ploughed winter-feeding lichen areas have been transformed into weak late-summer ranges. Forests of lichen-covered trees, extensively used as feeding grounds by reindeer during the hard snow-cover periods, vanished. In open felled areas, snow conditions are different from those in a sheltered forest, and digging for food becomes much more difficult. This change in grazing conditions has made the winter grazing of the reindeer much more difficult.

The winter grazing grounds dwindled and were no longer able to provide herding associations with a healthy annual rhythm for the reindeer. As this rhythm broke down, the balanced relationship between man and reindeer also disintegrated. The main point of the change in the man-reindeer relationship has been the transition from a relationship of equality to one of domination by man. Prior to this change, reindeer herding was the dominant feature of the Sami mode of life. After the change, the reindeer economy became an occupation. The change is remarkable from the viewpoint of the Sami ecosystem. Herding activities became mechanical, almost putting an end to the natural reindeer herding culture.

In the 1980s a huge national park was established in the eastern part of the area. In principle it should have been able to provide more protection for the traditional way of living of the local Sami reindeer. In practice the park has become an El Dorado for hikers, who damage the sensitive sub-Arctic ecosystem by disturbing the natural rhythm of the reindeer, trampling their grazing grounds underfoot.

The creation of environmentally protected areas in the Sami region also includes some colonialistic characteristics. From the viewpoint of the emerging autonomy of the Sami and other indigenous nations, we can see the seeds of conflict in the legislatures. In Finland, under the Nature Protection Act currently in force, nature reserves can be established only in areas owned by the state. We know that there are no state-owned lands in the territories of the former Lapp villages, but in fact more than 50 percent of the land of Sapmi in Finland is either nature reserve or wilderness, which are very similar in legal status. If the present legislation implies state ownership as a prerequisite for the establishment of nature reserves or aims at defining them as state-owned lands, the Sami will find themselves in a very complicated and contradictory situation.

To advance protection of nature as a primary condition of Sami life would mean to support state efforts to strengthen, perhaps finally, its rights to the former territories of the Lapp villages. On the other hand, if the Sami want to retain their voice and power in those areas and oppose the establishment of nature reserves, this means giving free reign to economic expansion and the exploitation of falls, waters, and wild forests.

It was the Chernobyl disaster of 1986 that served as a turning point in the Sami stand on environmental issues. Since then, the Sami people have been forced to consider the possibility of an ecocatastrophe, even in virginal Lapland (though the real impact of nuclear fallout was far worse in the 1960s after the Soviet nuclear tests in Novaya Zemlya).

A Sami environmental program was developed in cooperation with the Nordic Sami Council and adopted by the Nordic Sami Conference in Are, Sweden, in August 1986. The program declares, inter alia, that the Sami people have an irrevocable right "to take good care for our livelihoods and our communities according to our common provisions; together we are going to protect our lands, waters, resources, and our national inheritance for future generations." It calls for legal protection of Sami rights to land and natural resources and introduces a broad concept of "environment," which takes into account social and physical factors, with the latter subdivided into natural and cultural sectors.

Now, in the 1990s, the Sami people, together with other indigenous Arctic peoples and governments, have started work to protect the Arctic—to combat pollution, to safeguard the vital rights of the indigenous peoples, and to benefit the Arctic environment, a vulnerable and indispensable part of our common Mother Earth.

Designed by Thomas Christensen
Typeset by Philip Bronson
Printed by R. R. Donnelley & Sons